DYLAN THOMAS: A BIBLIOGRAPHY

Dylan Thomas

DYLAN THOMAS

A Bibliography

BY

J. ALEXANDER ROLPH

FOREWORD BY
DAME EDITH SITWELL

Illustrated with
sixteen pages of plates

GREENWOOD PRESS, PUBLISHERS
WESTPORT, CONNECTICUT

Library of Congress Cataloging in Publication Data

Rolph, John Alexander.
  Dylan Thomas: a bibliography.

  Reprint of the 1956 ed. published by J. M. Dent,
London, and New Directions, New York.
    1. Thomas, Dylan, 1914-1953--Bibliography.
Z8870.5.R6 1974   016.821'9'12   73-19568
ISBN 0-8371-7294-2

Originally published in 1956 by J. M. Dent & Sons Ltd., London;
New Directions, New York

Reprinted with the permission of New Directions Publishing
Corporation

Reprinted in 1974 by Greenwood Press,
a division of Williamhouse-Regency Inc.

Library of Congress Catalog Card Number 73-19568

ISBN 0-8371-7294-2

Printed in the United States of America

FOR

LEE

Contents

Illustrations

Dylan Thomas:
Biographical Notes

Born at Swansea, 22nd October 1914.

Educated at Swansea Grammar School, 1925–31. (First poem to be published in the school magazine: 1925.)

Reporter for the *South Wales Evening Post*, 1931–2.

Moved to London, 1933. (First publication in the London press: September 1933.)

Married Caitlin Macnamara and moved to Laugharne, Carmarthenshire, 1936.

First broadcast for the B.B.C., 1937.

Won the Oscar Blumenthal Prize offered by *Poetry* (Chicago), 1938.

Moved to Oxfordshire for a few months, then to London, 1940. Remained in London throughout the war, apart from brief sojourns at Laugharne, and New Quay, Cardigan. After the war, moved back to Oxfordshire.

Visited Italy, 1947.

Moved to the 'Boat House,' Laugharne, 1948.

Lecture tour, U.S.A., 1950 (February–June).

Collected Poems, 1934–52, awarded the William Foyle Poetry Prize for 1952 (**20th** January 1953), and the Etna-Taormina International Prize in Poetry, 1953.

Televised, 10th August 1953 (reading 'A Story'), B.B.C.

Left England for U.S.A., October 1953, to lecture and to meet Igor Stravinsky in connection with the libretto for an opera.

Died, New York, 9th November 1953.

Buried in St Martin's Churchyard, Laugharne, 24th November 1953.

Foreword:

The Young Dylan Thomas

by Edith Sitwell

AND so he remained, to the last day when I saw him, about three months before his death.

He was about to go to America, and he, his wife, and a great friend of his, the American poet Theodore Roethke, and *his* wife, lunched with me, to say good-bye. Alas, seeing him so gay (he spent most of the time teasing me about ridiculous remarks he had invented and put into my mouth) and looking so well, how could one have guessed for how long that good-bye would be.

I keep no diary, and have but little memory, so I cannot recollect the exact date when I saw him first. But it was in the autumn following his twenty-second birthday.

I had not seen his first book—I was living in Spain when it appeared, and it received few reviews, so I did not hear of it. But immediately on seeing the second book, I wrote to him, and, shortly afterwards, reviewed it at great length in the *Sunday Times*. The review was followed by about two months of virulent abuse of him in letters to the *Sunday Times*, which I had the pleasure of answering. The attackers got at least as good as they gave, and the air still echoes with the sound of numskulls being soundly hit.

As I say, I do not remember exactly on what day he came to see me first. It seems to me now, although I was so much his senior, that he and his great poetry were always a part of my life.

Poetry is, to some degree, the etheric body of the poet (though to some degree only)—so I will try to describe him physically.

He was not tall, but was extremely broad, and gave an impression of extraordinary strength, sturdiness, and super-abundant life. (His reddish-amber curls, strong as the curls

xiii

on the brow of a young bull, his proud, but not despising, bearing, emphasized this.)

In full face he looked much as William Blake must have looked as a young man. He had full eyes—like those of Blake—giving, at first, the impression of being unseeing, but seeing all, looking over immeasurable distances. To my mind, the only representation of him that gives his true likeness, his true character, is the photograph taken by the American photographer Mrs R. Thorne McKenna, that forms the cover of the February 1954 *Atlantic Monthly*.

I have never known anyone more capable of endearing himself to others. And this was not only the result of his great warmth, charm, and touching funniness. (He was a wonderful mimic, though never an unkind one.) He loved humanity, and had contempt only for the cruel, the unkind (these are not always identical), and the mean. He was most generous in his enthusiasms.

I never heard him say an unkind thing. (I admit that once, when a lady had kindly tried to teach him and me how to recite, he did, as soon as she left the room, draw his hand across his throat with a swift and most menacing gesture, making, at the same time, a face of really terrifying savagery.)

His death was followed by the most disgusting exhibition of mass hysteria it has ever been my misfortune to encounter. I do not, naturally, refer to the nation-wide mourning for him. That was proper, and to the nation's credit. I refer to the nauseating attempts of people who had, perhaps, once sat next him in a bar, to pretend they were his great friends, and to the output of bad verse addressed to him by incompetent versifiers who hoped, thus, to muscle in on his fame. I refer still more to what has come to be known as 'the Dylan legend.'

It is no doubt comforting to a certain kind of mind to see a great poet dragged down to their level, but it is not an agreeable sight. I do not for a moment deny that he sometimes 'went wild,' but I, personally, never saw him behave in any way unbecoming a great poet—never saw him behave with anything but dignity.

All this hysteria, and 'the Dylan legend,' alternates with such exquisite taste as that of a person (I am, perhaps luckily, unable to remember his name) who, writing in a recent number of the

American *Saturday Review of Literature* devoted to recent English literature, told us of 'The Refusal to mourn the Death of Dylan Thomas' by another person of an equal eminence.   (I do not mean of an eminence equal to that of Dylan Thomas.)

That was written within eighteen months of Mr Thomas's death.   And his wife, mother, and three children are living.

Introduction

THIS book lists all the published writings of Dylan Thomas that I have been able to trace. Amongst the unpublished material therefore excluded are certain talks, film scripts and juvenilia as well as writings which exit only in MS.

The vast majority of the material in books by Thomas appeared earlier in periodicals. Whilst I shall be glad to receive details of any errors or omissions in this and any other respect, one instance will quickly be noticed where an omission appears to have occurred but where several checks and re-checks have failed to prove otherwise: this is in the case of *Twenty-Five Poems*, where the acknowledgment page refers to, amongst other periodicals, *John O'London's Weekly*. Exhaustive examination of the files of this paper revealed no contribution by Thomas, nor could any member of its staff account for or remember such a contribution, nor, again, could any of Thomas's friends or associates with whom I have been in correspondence. I can only suggest that the paper was mentioned in Thomas's book in mistake for the *New English Weekly*, which is not mentioned but which did, in fact, originally publish several of the poems.

In all sections order is chronological, but a finding to any proper name, book, periodical, title, or first line can be made via the Index, where item numbers of major entries are in italics.

As a general rule a bibliography finds its way only into the hands of collectors, librarians, booksellers, and other bibliographers. To others it must seem little more than a rather dull list of facts. I have attempted to alleviate this situation somewhat in this book by moistening the material wherever possible—mostly in the case of the early books—with such extra-bibliographical history as has seemed worth recording. There is also a special, and strictly unbibliographical, section on Thomas's poems (section A) giving details of the changes that have taken place textually, if any, in each individual poem between its earliest and latest printings. Similar details are given in respect of prose writings, but these did not appear to warrant a special section on the same lines and will be found wherever relevant in section C and occasionally elsewhere.

I have been grateful for the generous help of the many friends and correspondents who have assisted during the compilation of this book. To any whose names do not, by chance, appear below I offer my sincerest apologies.

First and foremost I am indebted to Mr E. F. Bozman of J. M. Dent & Sons Ltd, and to Mr H. A. Roberts and Mr C. W. Hardy of the same firm, and to Mr James Laughlin IV and Mr Robert MacGregor of New Directions.

I should also like to thank Mr Leslie Rees, Chief Librarian, Swansea Central Library, and Mr Stanley Yonge, Reference Librarian, for their tireless assistance. Mr Yonge has been responsible for most of the research upon which the Dylan Thomas collection at the Library is founded.

For further invaluable help I should like to thank the Trustees of the Estate of the late Dylan Thomas, especially Mr David Higham, of Pearn, Pollinger & Higham, and Mr Wynford Vaughan Thomas; also Mr Henry Miller, Mr George Reavey, Mr David Archer, Mr Derek Stanford, Mr Constantine Fitz-gibbon, Miss Rosalind Wade, Miss Pamela Hansford Johnson, Mr John Hayward, Dr Daniel Jones, Mr Aneirin Talfan Davies, Mr Cecil Woolf, Miss Elizabeth Smart, Mr John D. Acquier, Mr Mark Goulden, Mr Herbert Howarth, Mr Alan Hodge, Mr Kenneth Allott, Mr Dante Thomas, Mr Ian Sharpe, Miss Brenda Chamberlain, Mr Gerald Bagley, Mr G. O. Physick, Mr George Scurfield, Mr Ralph Abercrombie, Mrs Louis Henry Cohn of House of Books Ltd, New York City, Mr Herbert Cahoon of the Pierpont Morgan Library, and Mr J. C. Hodgart, M.A.; also Messrs John Lane The Bodley Head Ltd, Jonathan Cape Ltd, Faber & Faber Ltd, The Favil Press Ltd, the Leighton-Straker Bookbinding Co. Ltd, J. D. Lewis & Sons Ltd, Readers Union Ltd, Putnam & Co. Ltd, the Knole Park Press Ltd, Mr William Griffiths of Griff's Ltd, The Argo Record Co. Ltd, Bertram Rota Ltd, the British Broadcasting Corporation, the *Daily Telegraph*, the *Sunday Times*, and the Director and staff of the British Museum.

Thanks are also due to Mr Vernon Watkins, who elaborated

Boat House
Laugharne
Carmarthenshire
October 9th 1952

Dear Mr Ralph,

Thank you very much for your letter. Indeed, I remember your talking to me about a bibliography of my writings — how could I forget? it seems such a fantastic project — and I'm glad, & amazed, it's actually made progress. Yes, ofcourse, I'll help you all I can about dates & placings of early poems etc, but I must warn you I won't remember much. I know I did quite a lot for the New English Weekly — poems & stories — which I've never gathered together or reprinted. But, anyway, I'll do all I can, & I'm sure it can be done by correspondence.

I'm very grateful to you for the trouble you are taking — such a peculiar cause, & for your very nice letter.

very sincerely,
Dylan Thomas

Thomas's first letter to the author

for me on the subject of Thomas's last poem; to Mr H. A. Clodd, who kindly loaned his copy of *18 Poems* for the purpose of illustration and assisted in other details; to Mr Ian Fleming, who now owns the original of Thomas's first letter to me and by whose courtesy a facsimile is here reproduced; to Mr Tristram Hull for the photograph facing page 11, and to Mr Ruthven Todd whose tireless and whole-hearted assistance it is impossible to measure.

I should like especially to acknowledge the kind help of Miss Runia Sheila MacLeod, who not only supplied numerous details of Thomas's earliest work in the London press but also gave me far more biographical information about this early period than I dared ask for, which in turn led me to many other sources of material.

I also extend warmest gratitude to Dame Edith Sitwell, for her foreword.

1956   J. A. R.

Literary Biographies of Poems by Dylan Thomas from September 1933 (London) to 1956

Introduction

THE primary aim of this section is to show the textual history of each of Thomas's poems composed within the major period of his literary career and indicate, as far as objective, factual evidence will allow, the development of his poetic craftsmanship and methods of revision.

The printings mentioned of each poem are not only the first and first in book form, therefore, but also, where they occur, any others where the text varies from either of these. The many printings that exist but do not fall into one of these three categories are not mentioned, though a departure from this is represented by the quotation of page numbers in *Collected Poems*—which do not denote altered versions except where stated but are given to facilitate quick reference.

The poems are arranged chronologically, each item being headed by the poem's title, followed, in brackets, by the first line. Where a poem has no title, or is entitled with the first line or part of it, or the title is simply 'Poem,' the first line is used. In all cases, the object of the headings being easy recognition, the best-known—usually the latest—version is used. Earlier titles, if any, are of course referred to within each history and can in any case be located via the Index.

Abbreviations used in Section A

Periodicals

Cont.P.P.—*Contemporary Poetry and Prose*
Cr.—The *Criterion*
Lis.—The *Listener*
L.L.T.—*Life and Letters Today*
N.E.W.—The *New English Weekly*
N.V.—*New Verse*
S.B.—The *Scottish Bookman*

S.R.—The *Sunday Referee*
20th C.V.—*Twentieth Century Verse*
V.S.—The *Voice of Scotland*
Y.P.—The *Year's Poetry*

Books (by Dylan Thomas)

C.P.—*Collected Poems*
D.E.—*Deaths and Entrances*
18 P.—*Eighteen Poems*
I.C.S.—*In Country Sleep*
M.L.—The *Map of Love*
N.P.—*New Poems*
25 P.—*Twenty-Five Poems*
26 P.—*Twenty-Six Poems*

A. 1 'No man believes who, when a star falls shot'

First appeared in *Adelphi*, Vol. 6, No. 6, Sept. 1933, p. 398.
4 verses of 6, 6, 5, and 7 lines.
Not so far reprinted.

A. 2   'That Sanity Be Kept'
('That sanity be kept I sit at open windows')

First appeared in the *Sunday Referee*, 3rd Sept. 1933, in 'Poets' Corner.'
5 verses of 6, 4, 2, 8, and 3 lines.
Not so far published in book form, but reprinted in *Adam*, Year 21,
No. 238, 1953, p. 17.

A. 3 'The force that through the green fuse drives the flower'

First appeared in the *Sunday Referee*, 29th Oct. 1933, in 'Poets' Corner,'
entitled 'Poem.'
First book form: *18 P.*, as poem 'Five,' p. 17, but with the following
differences:

	S.R.	18 P.
v. 4, l. 3	make her well	calm her sores
v. 4, l. 4	the timeless clouds	a weather's wind
v. 4, l. 5	That time is all.	How time has ticked a heaven round the stars.

S.R.—4 verses of 5, 5, 10, and 2 lines.
18 P.—5 verses of 5, 5, 5, 5, and 2 lines.

French trans. by Hélène Bokanowski in *Fontaine* (Alger), No. 25; Nov.–Dec. 1942, pp. 544–5.
C.P. p. 9, same as *18 P*. but first line as title.

A. 4   'Song'
                  ('Love me, not as the dreaming nurses')

First appeared in the *Sunday Referee*, 7th Jan. 1934, in 'Poets' Corner.'
4 verses of 4 lines each.
Not so far published in book form, but reprinted in *Adam*, Year 21, No. 238, 1953, p. 18.

A. 5   'Out of the Pit'
                  ('Within his head revolved a little world')

First appeared in the *New English Weekly*, Vol. 4, No. 15, 25th Jan. 1934, pp. 342–3.
16 verses of 5, 7, 5, 6, 9, 6, 6, 4, 4, 6, 4, 9, 10, 8, 5, and 10 lines.
Not so far reprinted.

A. 6   'A process in the weather of the heart'

First appeared in the *Sunday Referee*, 11th Feb. 1934, in 'Poets' Corner,' entitled 'Poem.'
First book form: *18 P.*, as poem 'Three,' p. 14, but with the following differences:

	S.R.	18 P.
v. 1, *l.* 3	grave	tomb
v. 2, *l.* 2	blindness,	blindness;

5 verses of 6, 3, 6, 3, and 6 lines.
C.P. p. 6, same as *18 P*. but first line as title.

A. 7   'The Woman Speaks'
                  ('No food suffices but the food of death;')

First appeared in *Adelphi*, Vol. 7, No. 6, Mar. 1934, pp. 399–400.
11 verses of 9, 8, 5, 4, 5, 5, 4, 6, 8, 4, and 6 lines.
Not so far reprinted.

A. 8   'Light breaks where no sun shines'

First appeared in the *Listener*, Vol. 11, No. 270, 14th Mar. 1934, p. 462, entitled 'Light.'

First book form: *The Year's Poetry* (1934), London, John Lane The Bodley Head, 1934, pp. 133–4.

Later (a few days) in *18 P.*, as poem 'Fourteen,' p. 30, but with the following minor differences:

	Lis. and Y.P.	*18 P.*
v. 1, *l.* 4	glow-worms	glowworms
v. 3, *l.* 4	fenced	fenced,

5 verses of 6 lines each.

French trans. by Hélène Bokanowski in *Fontaine* (Alger), No. 25, Nov.–Dec. 1942, pp. 546–7.

C.P. pp. 24–5, same as *18 P.* but first line as title and 'glow-worms' as originally.

A. 9   'Where once the waters of your face'

First appeared in the *Sunday Referee*, 25th Mar. 1934, in 'Poets' Corner,' entitled 'Poem.'

First book form: *18 P.*, as poem 'Seven,' p. 19, but with the following differences:

	S.R.	*18 P.*
v. 2, *l.* 6	salt fruits	wet fruits
v. 3, *l.* 2	love-beds	lovebeds

4 verses of 6 lines each.

C.P. p. 11, same as *18 P.* but first line as title.

A. 10   'Our eunuch dreams, all seedless in the light'

First appeared in *New Verse*, No. 8, Apr. 1934, pp. 11–12, untitled.

First book form: *18 P.*, as poem 'Nine,' pp. 22–3, but with the following differences:

	N.V.	*18 P.*
v. 2	The brides return (. . . etc., 4 lines)	The shades of girls (. . . etc., 4 quite different lines)
v. 4, *l.* 1	skulls	skull
v. 5, *l.* 1	my two	our two

8 verses; divided into 4 parts numbered I–IV, each part having two verses of 6 and 4 lines each.

C.P. pp. 14–15, same as *18 P.* but entitled 'Our eunuch dreams.'

A. 11   'When once the twilight locks no longer'

First appeared in *New Verse*, No. 9, June 1934, pp. 6–8, entitled 'One'
(being the first of two).

First book form: *18 P.*, as poem 'Two,' pp. 12–13, but with the
following differences:

	N.V.	18 P.
v. 2, l. 5	Which, sewn	That, sewn
v. 3, l. 6	doublecrossed his getter	drowned his father's magics
	with a dream	in a dream
v. 4, l. 2	red-haired	redhaired
v. 4, l. 3	drown their	filmed their
v. 5, l. 2	Sargossa	Sargasso
v. 5, l. 3	its dust	its dead
v. 7, l 5,	turnip shape	carcass shape
v. 8, l. 4	the dark	the light

8 verses of 6 lines each.

C.P. pp. 4–5, as *18 P.* but with verse 6 completely omitted and first
line as title.

A. 12   'I see the boys of summer in their ruin'

First appeared in *New Verse*, No. 9, June 1934, pp. 8–9, entitled 'Two'
(being the second of two).

First book form: *18 P.*, as poem 'One,' pp. 9–11, but with the
following differences:

	N.V.	18 P.
v. 1, l. 3	harvest	harvest,
v. 4, l. 2	shifting	shifting,
v. 4, l. 4	dog-dayed	dogdayed
v. 4, l. 5	doubt and dark	love and light
v. 5, l. 3	where punctual as death	where, punctual as death,
v. 5, l. 4	There in his night	There, in his night,
v. 8, l. 2	Heigh-ho	Heigh ho

9 verses of 6 lines each.   The poem is in 3 parts numbered I–III:
Parts I and II, 4 verses each; Part III, 1 verse.

C.P. pp. 1–3, same as *18 P.* but entitled 'I see the boys of summer.'

A. 13   'If I were tickled by the rub of love'

First appeared in *New Verse*, No. 10, Aug. 1934, pp. 8–9, entitled
'Poem.'

First book form: *18 P.*, as poem 'Eight,' pp. 20–1, same as *N.V.* except that in *l.* 1 *N.V.* has 'was tickled' and *18 P.* 'were tickled'. The 'was' version did, however, appear in book form, in *New Verse— An Anthology*, ed. G. Grigson, London, Faber & Faber Ltd, 1939, even though acknowledgment is made in that book to the Parton Press for permission to reprint from *18 P.*

7 verses of 7 lines each.

C.P. pp. 12–13, same as *18 P.* but first line as title.

A. 14   'From love's first fever to her plague, from the soft second'

First appeared in the *Criterion*, Vol. 14, No. 54, Oct. 1934, pp. 27–8, entitled 'Poem.'

First book form: *18 P.*, as poem 'Twelve,' pp. 27–8, but with the following differences:

	Cr.	18 P.
v. 2, *l.* 2	hatching	breaking
v. 2, *l.* 6	gray	grey
v. 3, *l.* 3	gland;	gland,
v. 3, *l.* 6	light;	light.
v. 3.	(*ll.* 7–8)	(omitted)
v. 3, *l.* 10	fellow;	fellow,
v. 4, *l.* 1	slowly;	slowly,
v. 5, *l.* 6	words'	word's
v. 7, *l.* 2	suck,	suck
v. 7, *l.* 4	two framed	two-framed
v. 7, *l.* 6	eye.	eye;

Cr.—7 verses of 9, 7, 11, 6, 8, 3, and 9 lines.

18 P.—7 verses of 9, 7, 9, 6, 8, 3, and 9 lines.

C.P. pp. 20–1, same as *18 P.* but with *l.* 3 of *v.* 2 omitted, and entitled 'From love's first fever to her plague.'

C.P.—7 verses of 9, 6, 9, 6, 8, 3, and 9 lines.

A. 15   'Poem in October'
('Especially when the October wind')

First appeared in the *Listener*, Vol. 12, No. 302, 24th Oct. 1934, p. 691.

First book form: *18 P.*, as poem 'Ten,' p. 24, same as *Lis.*

4 verses of 8 lines each.

C.P. pp. 16–17, same as *18 P.* but first line as title—presumably, in this case, to avoid confusion with the 1945 poem of the same name beginning 'It was my thirtieth year to heaven', though the earlier poem still seems to be referred to most often as 'Poem in October.'

A. 16   'Foster the light, nor veil the manshaped moon,'

First appeared in the *Sunday Referee*, 28th Oct. 1934, in 'Poets' Corner.' The first line here read 'Foster the light, nor veil the feeling moon,' and the poem consisted of:

4 verses of 6 lines each.   (Title: 'Poem.')

For reasons which may perhaps be inferred from the note of the second version, below, the poem escaped inclusion in *18 P.* nor has it appeared so far in book form elsewhere.

The second version first appeared in *Contemporary Poetry and Prose*, No. 1, May 1936, pp. 2–3, and although the first line contained only the one word change as shown above, the remaining lines were all rewritten.   The skeleton of the original remained in that the parts of speech appeared in the same positions, but the syntax was almost entirely different.   In addition a further verse was added making:

5 verses of 6 lines each.   (No title.)

First book form: *25 P.*, p. 31, untitled, same as *Cont.P.P.*

C.P. pp. 60–1, same as *25 P.* but with a comma at the end of *l.* 1, *v.* 5, and entitled 'Foster the light.'

A. 17   'Half of the fellow father as he doubles'

First appeared in *New Verse*, No. 12, Dec. 1934, pp. 10–12, entitled 'Poem.'

First book form (a few days later): *18 P.*, as poem 'Seventeen,' pp. 33–4, but with the following differences:

	N.V.	*18 P.*
v. 1, *l.* 4	To morrow's	To-morrow's
v. 2, *l.* 5	is planted	was planted
v. 4, *l.* 2	wood;	wood,
v. 4, *l.* 4	hair:	hairs;
v. 7, *l.* 2	rattles	rattled
v. 8, *l.* 2	south	South
v. 8, *l.* 3	deadhouse	dead house
v. 10, *l.* 1	what	What

In 2 parts, numbered 'I' and 'II,' each having 5 verses of 6 lines each.

C.P. pp. 30–2, same as *18 P.* but entitled 'My world is pyramid' (the opening words of Part 'II').

A. 18   'Before I knocked and flesh let enter,'

First appeared in *18 P.*, as poem 'Four,' pp. 15–16.
   8 verses of 6, 6, 6, 6, 6, 6, 6, and 4 lines.
   C.P. pp. 7–8, entitled 'Before I knocked,' same as *18 P.*

A. 19   'My hero bares his nerves along my wrist'

First appeared in *18 P.*, as poem 'Six,' p. 18.
   4 verses of 5 lines each.
   C.P. p. 10, entitled 'My hero bares his nerves,' same as *18 P.*

A. 20   'When, like a running grave, time tracks you down,'

First appeared in *18 P.*, as poem 'Eleven,' p. 25.
   10 verses of 5 lines each.
   C.P. pp. 18–19, entitled 'When, like a running grave,' same as *18 P.*

A. 21   'In the beginning was the three-pointed star,'

First appeared in *18 P.*, as poem 'Thirteen,' p. 29.
   5 verses of 6 lines each.
   C.P. pp. 22–3, entitled 'In the beginning,' same as *18 P.*

A. 22   'I fellowed sleep who kissed me in the brain,'

First appeared in *18 P.*, as poem 'Fifteen,' p. 31.
   6 verses of 5 lines each.
   C.P. pp. 26–7, entitled 'I fellowed sleep' and with the apostrophe before 'planing-heeled,' *v.* 1, *l.* 4, dropped, otherwise same as *18 P.*

A. 23   'I dreamed my genesis in sweat of sleep, breaking'

First appeared in *18 P.*, as poem 'Sixteen,' p. 32.
   7 verses of 4 lines each.
   C.P. pp. 28–9, entitled 'I dreamed my genesis,' same as *18 P.*

A. 24   'All all and all the dry worlds lever,'

First appeared in *18 P.*, as poem 'Eighteen,' pp. 35–6.

6 verses of 6 lines each, the whole poem divided into 3 parts numbered I–III of 2 verses each.

C.P. pp. 33–4, first line as title, same as *18 P.*

A. 25   'Poet: 1935'
('See, on gravel paths under the harpstrung trees,')

First appeared in the *Herald of Wales*, No. 6, 746, 8th June 1935, p. 1.

5 verses of 19, 4, 7, 11, and 10 lines.

This poem has not so far been reprinted *in toto*, but the first 8 lines appear in the first version of the broadcast 'Reminiscences of Childhood,' published in the *Listener*, 25th Feb. 1943, pp. 246–7, and reprinted in *Quite Early One Morning* (the book), pp. 1–7. In this prose piece is recorded the poem's childhood background, but immediately preceding the extract from the poem itself Thomas remarks: 'I wrote then, in a poem never to be published:'. It seems unlikely that such a lapse of memory could have occurred concerning a poem which, from its title, is presumed to have been written only eight years earlier—at a time when much of the poet's best-known work appeared (and Thomas's memory for such matters was a good deal better than is generally supposed). More probably it was composed, as the 'Reminiscences' suggest, some few years earlier; the syntax and style of the poem suggest this also.

A. 26   'Incarnate devil in a talking snake,'

First appeared in the *Sunday Referee*, 11th Aug. 1935, in 'Poets' Corner,' entitled 'Poem for Sunday.'

First book form: *25 P.*, p. 8, untitled and with the following differences:

	S.R.	25 P.
v. 1, *l.* 2	garden,	garden
v. 1, *l.* 5	god	God
v. 1, *l.* 6	thunder's hill	heavens' hill
v. 2, *l.* 4	Eastern	eastern
v. 3, *l.* 1	eden . . . guardians	Eden . . . guardian
v. 3, *l.* 2	harden.	harden,

3 verses of 6 lines each.

C.P. p. 40, same as *25 P.* but with the comma after 'garden' in *v.* 1, *l.* 2, and entitled 'Incarnate Devil.'

A. 27   'I, in my intricate image, stride on two levels,'

First appeared in *New Verse*, No. 16, Aug.–Sept. 1935, pp. 2–5, entitled 'A Poem in Three Parts.'

   First book form: 25 P., pp. 1–6, untitled and with the following differences:

	N.V.	*25 P.*
v. 1, *l.* 6	man iron	man-iron
v. 2, *l.* 2	spinning wheel	spinning wheels
v. 4, *l.* 2	bone-railed	bonerailed
v. 5, *l.* 1	trees,	trees
v. 8, *l.* 2	Cadaverous . . . thickly	cadaverous . . . thick
v. 8, *l.* 3	sea-bear	seabear
v. 8, *l.* 4	long tides	long sea
v. 9, *l.* 5	mask in	mask and
v. 9, *l.* 6	funeral.	funeral;
v. 10, *l.* 2	officers,	officers
v. 10, *l.* 4	cock on a dunghill	cock-on-a-dunghill
v. 11, *l.* 5	whole weed	whole-weed
v. 13, *l.* 5	topsy turvies	topsy-turvies
v. 16, *l.* 5	He, in	I, in
v. 18, *l.* 4	minerals.	mineral.

   18 verses of 6 lines each. In 3 parts, numbered I–III, of 6 verses each.

   C.P. pp. 35–8, same as 25 P. but entitled 'I, in my intricate image,'.

A. 28   'Do you not father me, nor the erected arm'

First appeared in the *Scottish Bookman*, Vol. 1, No. 2, Oct. 1935, p. (78), entitled 'Poem.'

   First book form: 25 P., pp. 15–16, untitled and with the following differences:

	S.B.	*25 P.*
v. 2, *l.* 7	fronts	front
v. 4, *l.* 2	sister's	sisters'

   4 verses of 8 lines each.

   C.P. pp. 46–7, same as 25 P. but entitled 'Do you not father me.'

A. 29   'A grief ago'

First appeared in *Programme*, No. 9, 23rd Oct. 1935, pp. (10)–(12), entitled 'Poem.'

Dylan and Caitlin Thomas
circa 1935

First book form: 25 P., pp. 25–6, untitled and with the following
minor differences:

	Programme	25 P.
v. 2, l. 1	grief?	grief,
v. 2, l. 3	finger-man	fingerman
v. 4, l. 2	peoples sea	people's sea
v. 5, l. 7	gypsy	gipsy

5 verses of 8 lines each.
C.P. pp. 54–5, same as 25 P., first line as title.

A. 30   'How soon the servant sun'

First appeared in Programme, No. 9, 23rd Oct. 1935, pp. (2)–(3),
entitled 'Poem.'
    First book form: 25 P., pp. 27–8, untitled and with the dashes in
verses 1, 2, and 4 replaced by brackets, and with the following further
variations of which the last is obviously merely a misprint:

	Programme	25 P.
v. 2, l. 6	. . . masters,	. . . masters, as his strange
v. 2, l. 7	As his strange his strange	Man morrow. . . (etc.)
v. 2, l. 8	Man marrow . . . (etc.)	(no 8th line)
v. 3, l. 3	mouses' bane	mouse's bone

Programme: 5 verses of 7, 8, 7, 7, and 6 lines.
25 P.: 5 verses of 7, 7, 7, 7, and 6 lines.
C.P. pp. 56–7, same as 25 P., first line as title.

A. 31   'Altarwise by owl-light in the half-way house'

This poem, together with the six sonnets that follow (A. 32–A. 37),
first appeared in Life and Letters Today, Vol. 13, No. 2, Dec. 1935,
pp. 73–5, each poem being numbered, I–VII, and the whole headed
'Poems for a Poem.'   In the 'Notes on Contributors' to this number
part of a letter which accompanied the MS. is quoted, in which Thomas
expressed the hope that the editors would 'like it, despite its obscurity
and incompleteness.   It's the first passage of what's going to be a very
long poem indeed.'
    Only three more sonnets, however, were added (see A. 44, A. 45,
and A. 46) and the ten subsequently appeared as a sequence for the
first time in 25 P., pp. 42–7, which also constitutes the first appearance

of each poem in book form.   All the poems are of 14 lines each in all printings but a few minor alterations that have been made to the seven originally published in *L.L.T.* are outlined below under their individual headings.

'Altarwise by owl-light. . . .', sonnet 'I' (*L.L.T.*, p. 73) appeared unchanged in *25 P.* (p. 42), but in *C.P.*, where these opening words form the title of the whole sequence, the following minor differences occur, p. 71:

	25 P.	*C.P.*
l. 1	halfway-house	half-way house
l. 3	hang-nail	hangnail
l. 9	halfway	half-way
l. 12	shelter,	shelter:

It was this poem which Thomas 'explained' in some detail, in answer to Dame Edith Sitwell's criticism of it in her review of *25 P.* (see D. 17).

A. 32   'Death is all metaphors, shape in one history;'

See A. 31.
L.L.T. p. 73, as sonnet 'II.'
25 P. pp. 42–3, same as *L.L.T.*
C.P. pp. 71–2, same as *25 P.* but with a full stop at end of *l.* 10 in place of a semi-colon.

A. 33   'First there was the lamb on knocking knees'

See A. 31.
L.L.T. p. 43, as sonnet 'III.'
25 P. p. 43, same as *L.L.T.* but with no comma at end of first line.
C.P. p. 72, same as *25 P.*

A. 34   'What is the metre of the dictionary?'

See A. 31.
L.L.T. p. 74, as sonnet 'V.'
25 P. pp. 43–4, same as *L.L.T.* but with 'Love's a reflection' altered to 'Love's reflection' in *l.* 11.
C.P. pp. 72–3, same as *25 P.* except for *l.* 8, where 'crooked lad' has become 'crooked boy'.

A. 35   'And from the windy West came two-gunned Gabriel,'

See A. 31.
L.L.T. p. 74, as sonnet 'V.'
25 P. p. 44, with the following minor differences:

	L.L.T.	*25 P.*
l. 1	windy west	windy West
l. 5	Black tongued	Black-tongued
l. 6	in the night.	in the night;

C.P. p. 73 but with the full stop after 'night' in *l.* 6 as originally and a comma at end of *l.* 10 in place of a semi-colon.

A. 36   'Cartoon of slashes on the tide-traced crater,'

See A. 31.
L.L.T. pp. 74–5, as sonnet 'VI.'
25 P. pp. 44–5, same as *L.L.T.*
C.P. p. 74, same as *25 P.* but with full stop at end of *l.* 4 in place of a colon.

A. 37   'Now stamp the Lord's Prayer on a grain of rice,'

See A. 31.
L.L.T. p. 75, as sonnet 'VII.'
25 P. p. 45, with the following differences:

	L.L.T.	*25 P.*
l. 1	lord's prayer	Lord's Prayer
l. 2	bible-leaved	Bible-leaved
l. 8	seasawers, play on	sea-sawers, fix in
l. 10	beginning;	beginning.

C.P. pp. 74–5, same as *25 P.* but with a full stop at end of *l.* 5 in place of a semi-colon.

A. 38   'The hand that signed the paper felled a city;'

First appeared in *New Verse*, No. 18, Dec. 1935, pp. 15–16, as No. 'I' of 'Three Poems.'

c

First book form: 25 P., p. 33, untitled, with the following differences:

	N.V.	25 P.
v. 3, l. 2	grew	grew,
v. 4, l. 1	fingers crust	five kings count
v. 4, l. 2	wounds	wound
v. 4, l. 3	The hand	A hand

4 verses of 4 lines each.

C.P. p. 62, same as 25 P. but entitled 'The hand that signed the paper' and with 'pat the brow' in v. 4, l. 2 altered to 'stroke the brow'.

This poem was reprinted in La Nouvelle Saison (Paris), Vol. 1, No. 3, July 1938, together with a French trans. by 'Dillon Fitzgibbon' (Constantine Fitzgibbon), representing one of the earliest, if not the earliest, trans. into French of work by Thomas. (See C. 104.)

A. 39   'Should lanterns shine, the holy face,'

First appeared in New Verse, No. 18, Dec. 1935, p. 16, as No. 'II' of 'Three Poems.'

First book form: 25 P., p. 34, untitled, with the following differences:

	N.V.	25 P.
v. 2, l. 4	And when it quickens	And, when it quickens,
v. 2, l. 6	move,	move
v. 5	(total, 2 lines)	(omitted)

N.V.—5 verses of 8, 7, 2, 2, and 2 lines.
25 P.—4 verses of 8, 7, 2, and 2 lines.
C.P. p. 63, entitled 'Should lanterns shine,' same as 25 P.

A. 40   'I have longed to move away'

First appeared in New Verse, No. 18, Dec. 1935, pp. 16–17, as No. 'III' of 'Three Poems.'

First book form: 25 P., p. 35, untitled, with the following differences:

	N.V.	25 P.
v. 1, l. 3	terror's	terrors'
v. 2, l. 7	lips from	lips at
v. 2, l. 10	Half-convention	Half convention

2 verses of 10 lines each.

C.P. p. 64, first line as title, same as 25 P.

A. 41   'Grief thief of time crawls off,'

First appeared in *Comment*, Vol. 1, No. 9, 1st Feb. 1936, p. 66, entitled 'Poem.'

First book form: *25 P.*, p. 38, untitled, and with the following minor differences:

	Comment	25 P.
v. 1, *l.* 8	sea-light	sea light
v. 2, *l.* 5	an eunuch	a eunuch
v. 2, *l.* 8	to-day	to day
v. 2, *l.* 14	father's	fathers'

2 verses of 14 lines each.

C.P. p. 67, entitled 'Grief thief of time,' same as *25 P.*

This was the only poem contributed by Thomas to *Comment*, and also the only poem by him in *First 'Comment' Treasury*, London, Comment Press, 1937 (p. 77).

A. 42   'Hold hard, these ancient minutes in the cuckoo's month,'

First appeared in *Caravel* (Majorca), Vol. 2, No. 5, Mar. 1936, p. (15), untitled.

First book form: *25 P.*, p. 19, same as *Caravel*.

4 verses of 6 lines each.

C.P. p. 49, same as *25 P.*, first line as title.

A. 43   'Find meat on bones that soon have none,'

First appeared in *Purpose*, Vol. 8, No. 2, Apr.–June 1936, pp. 102–3, untitled.

First book form: *25 P.*, pp. 36–7, the following two differences amounting to no more than correction of misprints:

	Purpose	25 P.
v. 1, *l.* 1	Fine	Find
v. 1, *l.* 8	hags	rags

5 verses of 8, 8, 8, 8, and 9 lines.

C.P. pp. 65–6, entitled 'Find meat on bones' and with additional opening quotation marks at verses 2 and 4, otherwise same as *25 P.*

A. 44   'This was the crucifixion on the mountain,'

First appeared in *Contemporary Poetry and Prose*, No. 1, May 1936, p. 2, untitled.

First book form: *25 P.*, p. 46, as poem 'VIII' of the sonnet sequence (see A. 31) but with the following differences:

	Cont. P.P.	25 P.
l. 9	three-footed	three-coloured
l. 12	my skeleton	the skeleton

In addition to these variations *Cont.P.P.* has a break between lines 10 and 11 where *25 P.* has none.

Cont.P.P.—2 verses of 10 and 4 lines.

25 P.—1 verse of 14 lines.

French trans. by Hélène Bokanowski (*25 P.* version) in *Fontaine*, No. 25, Nov.–Dec. 1942, pp. 547–8, entitled 'La Crucifixion.'

C.P. p. 75, same as *25 P.*

A. 45   'From the oracular archives and the parchment,'

First appeared in *Contemporary Poetry and Prose*, No. 3, July 1936, p. 53, as poem 'I' of 'Two Poems Towards a Poem.'

First book form: *25 P.*, pp. 46–7, as poem 'IX' of the sonnet sequence (see A. 31), same as *Cont.P.P.*

1 verse of 14 lines.

C.P. pp. 75–6, same as *25 P.*

A. 46   'Let the tale's sailor from a Christian voyage'

First appeared in *Contemporary Poetry and Prose*, No. 3, July 1936, p. 53, as poem 'II' of 'Two Poems Towards a Poem.'

First book form: *25 P.*, p. 47, as poem 'X' of the sonnet sequence (see A. 31), same as *Cont.P.P.* but with 'rockbirds' in place of 'rock-birds', l. 4.

1 verse of 14 lines.

C.P. p. 76, same as *25 P.* but with 'half-way' in place of 'halfway', l. 2.

A. 47   'Why east wind chills and south wind cools'

First appeared in the *New English Weekly*, Vol. 9, No. 14, 16th July 1936, p. 270 as, 'I' of 'Two Poems.'

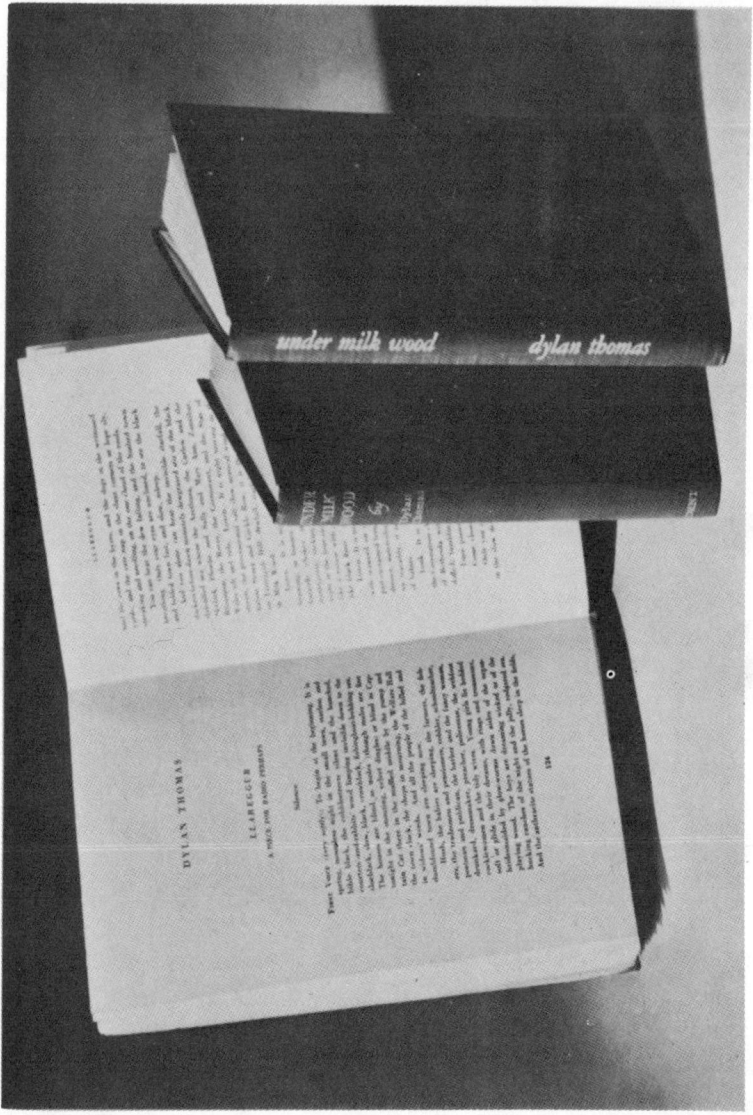

'Llareggub' (which later became the first part of 'Under Milk Wood') in *Botteghe Oscure* (C. 175), and UNDER MILK WOOD, English and American editions (B. 21 & 22)

First book form: *25 P.*, p. 23, untitled and with the following differences:

	N.E.W.	*25 P.*
v. 2, *l.* 6	roof-tops	rooftops
v. 3, *l.* 4	houses of the sky	towers of the skies

3 verses of 9, 6, and 11 lines.

C.P. p. 53, entitled 'Why east wind chills,' same as *25 P.*

A. 48   'This bread I break was once the oat,'

First appeared in the *New English Weekly*, Vol. 9, No. 14, 16th July 1936, p. 270, as 'II' of 'Two Poems.'

First book form: *25 P.*, p. 7, untitled and with a comma at end of *l.* 2, *v.* 2, where *N.E.W.* is unpunctuated.   There is also the misprint 'wind' for 'wine' in *25 P.*, *v.* 2, *l.* 1.   That this was a misprint is confirmed by Thomas in a letter to a correspondent (see *The Times Literary Supplement*, 10th Sept. 1954, p. 573).

3 verses of 5 lines each.

C.P. p. 39, entitled 'This bread I break' and with the misprint in *v.* 2, *l.* 1 corrected, otherwise same as *25 P.*

A. 49   'Before we mothernaked fall'

First appeared in the *New English Weekly*, Vol. 9, No. 16, 30th July 1936, p. 310, entitled 'Poem.'

2 verses of 8 lines each.

Not so far reprinted.

A. 50   'Was there a time when dancers with their fiddles'

First appeared in the *New English Weekly*, Vol. 9, No. 17/20, 3rd Sept. 1936, p. 328, entitled 'Poem.'

First book form: *25 P.*, p. 20, untitled and with the following differences:

	N.E.W.	*25 P.*
l. 4	put . . . maggots . . . track,	set . . . maggot . . . track.
l. 5	unsafe,	unsafe.
l. 8	hands, and as	hands, and, as
l. 9	unhurt	unhurt,

1 verse of 9 lines.

C.P. p. 50, entitled 'Was there a time,' same as *25 P.*

A. 51   'The seed-at-zero shall not storm'

First appeared in 25 P., pp. 10–12, untitled.
8 verses of 7 lines each.
C.P. pp. 42–3, entitled 'The seed-at-zero,' same as 25 P.

A. 52   'Shall gods be said to thump the clouds'

First appeared in 25 P., p. 13, untitled.
4 verses of 4, 3, 3, and 4 lines.
C.P. p. 44, first line as title, same as 25 P.

A. 53   'Here in this spring, stars float along the void;'

First appeared in 25 P., p. 14, untitled.
4 verses of 4, 4, 5, and 4 lines.
C.P. p. 45, entitled 'Here in this spring,' same as 25 P.

A. 54   'Out of the sighs a little comes,'

First appeared in 25 P., pp. 17–18, untitled.
4 verses of 9, 7, 7, and 6 lines.
French trans. by Jean Wahl in *Adam*, Year 21, No. 238, 1953, p. 42,
entitled 'Des Soupirs,' but with no break between verses 2 and 3.
C.P. p. 48, entitled 'Out of the sighs,' same as 25 P.

A. 55   'Now' ('/Say nay,/Man dry man,/' etc.)

First appeared in 25 P., pp. 21–2, untitled.
5 verses of 7 lines each.
C.P. pp. 51–2, entitled 'Now,' same as 25 P.

A. 56   'Ears in the turrets hear'

First appeared in 25 P., pp. 29–30, untitled.
5 verses of 9, 7, 9, 6, and 2 lines.
French trans. by G.-A. Astre in *Age Nouveau*, No. 49/50, May 1950,
pp. 66–7.
C.P. pp. 58–9, first line as title, same as 25 P.

A. 57   'And death shall have no dominion.'

First appeared in 25 P., p. 39, untitled.
   3 verses of 9 lines each.
   C.P. p. 68, first line as title, same as 25 P.

A. 58   'Then was my neophyte,'

First appeared in 25 P., pp. 40–1, untitled; but an earlier version
appeared about three weeks later in *Purpose*, Vol. 8, No. 4, Oct.–Dec.
1936, pp. 230–1, as the first of 'Two Poems.' Probably Thomas
effected the alterations to proofs of his book after having submitted the
poem to *Purpose*; that the version in 25 P. is the later is evidenced
by the identical version in C.P.   The variations are as follows (line
numbers are those of 25 P.):

	Purpose	25 P.
v. 3, l. 1	(line absent)	He films my vanity.
v. 3, l. 6	black, headless	masked, headless
v. 4, l. 5	From that	From your
v. 4, l. 10	heart	heart,

Purpose—4 verses of 12, 12, 11, and 12 lines.
25 P.—4 verses of 12 lines each.
   The *Purpose* version also appeared in *Transition*, No. 25, Fall 1936,
pp. 20–1.   Of these two periodicals it is not wholly certain which
appeared first; evidence points strongly to *Purpose*, though by only a
few days.
   C.P. pp. 69–70, first line as title, same as 25 P.

A. 59   'To-day, this insect, and the world I breathe,'

First appeared in 25 P., p. 9, untitled, but an earlier version appeared
in *Purpose*, Vol. 8, No. 4, Oct.–Dec. 1936, pp. 231–2, as the second of
'Two Poems,' rather later (see A. 58).   'Version' is perhaps here an
exaggeration, the first of the two minor differences being in any case
only a misprint:

	Purpose	25 P.
v. 1, l. 4	She dear	The dear
v. 5, l. 3	fib	fibs

5 verses of 8, 1, 8, 1, and 8 lines.
C.P. p. 41, entitled 'To-day, this insect,' same as 25 P.

A. 60   'We lying by seasand, watching yellow'

First appeared in *Poetry* (Chicago), Vol. 49, No. 4, Jan. 1937, p. 183, entitled 'We Lying By Seasand.'

First book form: *The Year's Poetry 1937*, London, John Lane The Bodley Head, 1937, p. 132, entitled 'Poem,' but here 'leave red rock', *l*. 20, has become 'drown red rock'.

Two further minor changes were made for *M.L.* (p. 8, untitled) as follows:

	Y.P.	M.L.
l. 17	gay seaside	gay, seaside
l. 22	off the rock	off rock

C.P. p. 82, entitled 'We lying by seasand,' same as *M.L.*

A. 61   'It is the sinners' dust-tongued bell claps me to churches'

First appeared in *Twentieth Century Verse*, No. 1, Jan. 1937, p. (3), entitled 'Poem, Part I.'

First book form: '*The Year's Poetry 1937*,' London, John Lane The Bodley Head, 1937, pp. 133–4, entitled 'Poem,' but here v. 5, *l*. 5 has 'plagued' in place of 'clapped'.

Later in *M.L.*, pp. 9–10, untitled, same as *Y.P.*

5 verses of 6 lines each.

C.P. pp. 83–4, entitled 'It is the sinners' dust-tongued bell,' same as *M.L.*

A. 62   'I make this in a warring absence when'

First appeared in *Twentieth Century Verse*, No. 8, Jan.–Feb. 1938, pp. (3)–(4), entitled 'Poem (for Caitlin).'

A version in *Delta*, Apr. 1938, pp. 6–7, varies only to the extent of three misprints.

Later in *Wales*, No. 5, Summer 1938, pp. 179–81, with *l*. 5 of v. 9 ('Once where . . .' etc.) omitted, though this may also be a printer's error as the line is replaced in all later printings.

First book form: *New Directions in Prose and Poetry 1938*, Norfolk, Conn., New Directions, 1938, as the third of 'Three Poems' (pages unnumbered), same as *20th C.V.*

Later in *M.L.*, pp. 4–7, untitled and with 'jaw-bone' (v. 5, *l*. 6) and 'sun-gloved' (v. 6, *l*. 8) where previously unhyphenated. Also here the break between verses 5 and 6 is two lines earlier.

20th C.V.—9 verses of 8, 7, 8, 7, 8, 7, 8, 7, and 8 lines.
Wales—9 verses of 8, 7, 8, 7, 8, 7, 8, 7, and 7 lines.
M.L.—9 verses of 8, 7, 8, 7, 6, 9, 8, 7, and 8 lines.
C.P. pp. 78–80, entitled 'I make this in a warring absence,' same as *M.L.*

A. 63   'The spire cranes.   Its statue is an aviary.'

First appeared in *Wales*, No. 4, Mar. 1938, p. 138, entitled 'Poem.'
    Later in *Poetry* (Chicago), Vol. 52, No. 5, Aug. 1938, p. 249, as the fourth of 'Four Poems,' with 'prison spire', *l. 5*, in place of 'prison statue'.
    First book form: *M.L.*, pp. 11–12, untitled, same as *Poetry*.
    1 verse of 11 lines.
    C.P. p. 86, entitled 'The spire cranes,' same as *M.L.*

A. 64   (In Memory of Ann Jones)
              ('After the funeral, mule praises, brays,')

First appeared in *Life and Letters Today*, Vol. 18, No. 12, Summer 1938, p. 45, entitled '(In Memory of Ann Jones).'
    First book form: *New Directions in Prose and Poetry 1938*, Norfolk, Conn., New Directions, 1938, as the first of 'Three Poems' (pages unnumbered), same as *L.L.T.* This book preceded *The Year's Poetry 1938* by nearly two months.
    Later in *M.L.*, pp. 12–13, same title but with the following minor differences:

	L.L.T., etc.	*M.L.*
l. 14	hooded	hooded,
l. 15	sun,	sun
l. 20	body.)	body).
l. 35	stone,	stone.
l. 36	cloud-sapped	cloud-sopped
l. 37	small voice	hewn voice
l. 38	for ever	forever

    1 verse of 40 lines.
    French trans. by Hélène Bokanowski and Armand Guibert in *Fontaine* (Alger), No. 37/40, 1944, pp. 441–3; another, by Claude Delmas, in *Adam*, Year 21, No. 238, 1953, p. 43.
    There is a separate version of this poem (see B. 8) as 'Caseg Broadsheet No. 5,' but here the first 9 lines are omitted and *l.* 25 (using the line numbers of the full version) reads 'ring and swing' in place

of 'sing and swing', even though permission to 'reprint' from *M.L.* is acknowledged.

C.P. pp. 87–8, entitled 'After the funeral (In Memory of Ann Jones),' same as *M.L.*

A. 65   'Not from this anger, anticlimax after'

First appeared in *Poetry* (Chicago), Vol. 52, No. 5, Aug. 1938, pp. 248–9, as the third of 'Four Poems.'

First book form: *M.L.*, pp. 14–15, untitled, with *l.* 4 having 'land strapped by hunger' in place of 'land without weather,'.

2 verses of 7 lines each (*Poetry*).

C.P. p. 90, entitled 'Not from this anger,' same as *M.L.* but without a break, making 1 verse of 14 lines.   (This latter alteration may have been made also for *M.L.*, but as the crucial point—*l.* 7—falls at the foot of p. 14 it is not possible to confirm this conclusively.)

A. 66   'O make me a mask and a wall to shut from your spies'

First appeared in *Poetry* (Chicago), Vol. 52, No. 5, Aug. 1938, p. 248, as the second of 'Four Poems.'

First book form: *M.L.*, p. 11, untitled, same as *Poetry*.

1 verse of 12 lines.

C.P. p. 85, entitled 'O make me a mask,' unchanged.

A. 67   'When all my five and country senses see,'

First appeared in *Poetry* (Chicago), Vol. 52, No. 5, Aug. 1938, p. 247, as the first of 'Four Poems.'

First book form: *M.L.*, p. 7, untitled and with the following differences:

	Poetry	*M.L.*
v. 1, *l.* 3	How through	How, through
v. 1, *l.* 7	wind and shell	breeze and shell
v. 1, *l.* 8	eyed tongue talk	lynx tongue cry
v. 1, *l.* 9	How her sweet	That her fond
v. 2, *l.* 2	watch awake;	grope awake;
v. 2, *l.* 3	falls on	drops on

In addition a completely different line is substituted at *v.* 1, *l.* 4. 2 verses of 10 and 4 lines.

C.P. p. 81, first line as title, same as *M.L.*

A. 68   'How shall my animal'

First appeared in the *Criterion*, Vol. 18, No. 70, Oct. 1938, pp. 29–30,
entitled 'Poem.'

   First book form: *New Directions in Prose and Poetry 1938*, Norfolk,
Conn., New Directions, 1938, as the second of 'Three Poems' (pages
unnumbered), same as *Criterion*.

   Later in *M.L.*, pp. 15–17, untitled, unchanged.

   4 verses of 11 lines each.

   C.P. pp. 91–2, first line as title, unchanged.

A. 69   'The tombstone told when she died.'

First appeared in *Seven*, No. 3, Winter 1938, p.17, entitled 'Poem.'

   Appeared shortly afterwards in the *Voice of Scotland*, Vol. 1, No. 3,
Dec. 1938–Feb. 1939, p. 12, but where *Seven* has '*Her* tombstone
told when she died', first line, *V.S.* has '*The* tombstone told *me* when
she died' (italics mine).   Also both versions have 3 verses and the
first line of the last verse reading '*winding* film' (italics mine).

   First book form ('Her . . .' version): *New Directions in Prose and Poetry
1939*, Norfolk, Conn., New Directions, 1939, p. 94, same as *Seven*.

   3 verses of 10 lines each.

   Later in *M.L.*, pp. 17–18, untitled and with 'The . . .', *l.* 1, and
'hurried film', first line of last verse.

   C.P. p. 93, first line as title, same as *M.L.* but arranged:

   2 verses of 20 and 10 lines.   (Though here, as A. 65, the change
in arrangement may have been made earlier as *l.* 10 falls at the foot of
the page in *M.L.*)

A. 70   'I, the first named, am the ghost of this sir and
                    christian friend'

First appeared in *Seven*, No. 3, Winter 1938, p. 17, entitled 'Poem.'

   1 verse of 4 lines.

   Not so far reprinted.

A. 71   'Twenty-four years remind the tears of my eyes'

First appeared in *Life and Letters Today*, Vol. 20, No. 16, Dec. 1938,
p. 42, entitled 'Birthday Poem.'

   First book form: *M.L.*, p. 24, untitled, same as *L.L.T.*

   1 verse of 9 lines.

   C.P. p. 99, entitled 'Twenty-four years,' same as *M.L.*

A. 72   'Because the pleasure-bird whistles after the hot wires,'

First appeared in *Twentieth Century Verse*, No. 15/16, Feb. 1939, p. 149, entitled 'January 1939.'
   First book form: *M.L.*, pp. 3–4, entitled '(January 1939),' same as *20th C.V.*
   1 verse of 25 lines.
   C.P. p. 77, entitled 'Because the pleasure-bird whistles,' unchanged.

A. 73   'Poem in the Ninth Month' ('A saint about to fall,')

First appeared in *Poetry* (London), No. 1, Feb. 1939, pp. (26)–(27), entitled 'Poem in the Ninth Month.'
   First book form: *M.L.*, pp. 19–21, untitled, same as *Poetry*.
   3 verses of 17 lines each.
   C.P. pp. 95–6, first line as title, unchanged.

A. 74   'On no work of words now for three lean months in the bloody'

First appeared in *Wales*, No. 6/7, Mar. 1939, p. 196, entitled 'Poem.'
   First book form: *M.L.*, pp. 18–19, untitled, same as *Wales*, but with v. 3, l. 1 having 'is pleasing death' in place of 'is a pleasing death'.
   4 verses of 3 lines each.
   C.P. p. 94, entitled 'On no work of words,' same as *M.L.*

A. 75   'Once it was the colour of saying'

First appeared in *Wales*, No. 6/7, Mar. 1939, p. 196, entitled 'Poem.'
   First book form: *M.L.*, p. 14, untitled and with the following differences:

	Wales	*M.L.*
l. 5	The seaslides	The gentle seaslides
l. 6	charmingly dead	charmingly drowned
l. 8	we stoned at night	at night we stoned
l. 12	undoing	undoing,

   1 verse of 13 lines.
   C.P. p. 89, first line as title, same as *M.L.*

COLLECTED POEMS—English edition, limited issue binding (B. 17)

A. 76 ' "If my head hurt a hair's foot" '

First appeared in *Poetry* (London), No. 2, Apr. 1939, p. (25), entitled 'Poem.'

First book form: *M.L.*, pp. 22–3, untitled and with the following minor differences:

	Poetry	*M.L.*
v. 4, *l.* 4	none, none, none	none, none, none,
v. 5, *l.* 2	for ever	forever

Also, in *Poetry* quotation marks open only at *v.* 1 and *v.* 4: in *M.L.* they open at each verse.

6 verses of 5 lines each.

C.P. pp. 97–8, first line as title, same as *M.L.*

A. 77 'To Others Than You'
('Friend by enemy I call you out.')

First appeared in *Seven*, No. 6, Autumn 1939, p. 5, as the first of 'Three Poems.'

First book form: *N.P.*, p. (6), same as *Seven*. Later in *D.E.*, p. 14, same as *Seven* but with 'That though', *l.* 18, in place of 'That, though' and with a break between lines 17 and 18.

Seven and *N.P.*—2 verses of 1 and 20 lines.

D.E. (and *C.P.*)—3 verses of 1, 16, and 4 lines.

C.P. p. 107, same as *D.E.*

A. 78 'Paper and Sticks'
('Paper and sticks and shovel and match')

First appeared in *Seven*, No. 6, Autumn 1939, p. 6, as the second of 'Three Poems.'

First book form: *D.E.*, p. 23, same as *Seven* but for 'navy blue', 'one pound', and 'silver spooned' (*ll.* 5, 9, and 15) which in 'Seven' were all hyphenated.

6 verses of 3 lines each.

Not in *C.P.* (but present in proof copies—see B.16).

A. 79 'When I woke, the town spoke.'

First appeared in *Seven*, No. 6, Autumn 1939, p. 7, as the third of 'Three Poems.'

First book form: *N.P.*, p. (8), entitled 'Poem.'

2 verses of 15 and 14 lines.

Later in *D.E.*, p. 40, entitled 'When I woke' and with the following differences:

	Seven	*D.E.*
v. 2, l. 4	death-staggered	death-stagged
v. 2, l. 5	Battering and no-account mammoth	Mammoth and sparrow-fall
v. 2, l. 10	air	air,

Beyond this point the last four lines of the *Seven* version are completely rewritten and one extra line added.

D.E.—2 verses of 15 lines each.

C.P. p. 134, same as *D.E.*

A. 80   'Unluckily for a death'

First appeared in *Life and Letters Today*, Vol. 23, No. 26, Oct. 1939, pp. 66–8, entitled 'Poem (to Caitlin)'.

First book form: *N.P.*, pp. (11)–(12).

Later in *D.E.*, pp. 16–17, entitled 'Unluckily for a Death,' with syntax about 80 per cent altered throughout and the last verse reduced by one line.

Seven and N.P.—4 verses of 14, 14, 14, and 15 lines.

D.E.—4 verses of 14 lines each.

C.P. pp. 109–10, same as *D.E.* but with 'duck-billed' in place of 'duck billed', v. 3, l. 5.

A. 81   'Once below a time'

First appeared in *Life and Letters Today*, Vol. 24, No. 31, Mar. 1940 (Welsh Number), pp. 274–5, entitled 'Poem.'

First book form: *N.P.*, pp. (21)–(22).

Not in *D.E.*

In 2 Parts, Part 'I' having 3 verses of 12, 6, and 10 lines, and Part 'II' 4 verses of 6, 6, 8, and 3 lines.

C.P. pp. 132–3, first line as title, same as *D.E.* but arranged: Part 'I' 2 verses of 12 and 16 lines, Part 'II' 3 verses of 6, 6, and 11 lines.

A. 82   'There was a saviour'

First appeared in *Horizon*, Vol. 1, No. 5, May 1940, pp. 318–19, entitled 'Poem.'

First book form: *New Poems 1942*, Mount Vernon, N.Y., Peter Pauper Press, 1942.

Later in *N.P.*, p. (1).

Later in *D.E.*, pp. 33–4, first line as title, with the following differences:

	Horizon, etc.	D.E.
v. 3, l. 5	On the ground	On to the ground
v. 4, l. 1	cry	cry,
v. 4, l. 2	side	side,
v. 4, l. 3	inhospitable, hollowed year,	inhospitable hollow year,
v. 4, l. 8	little-known	little known
v. 5, l. 7	our soft	the soft
v. 5, l. 8	silk-and-rough	silk and rough

5 verses of 8 lines each.
C.P. pp. 125–6, same as *D.E.*

A. 83 'The Countryman's Return'
('Embracing low-falutin')

First appeared in *Cambridge Front* (No. 1), Summer 1940, pp. 8–9.
4 verses of 25, 26, 25, and 25 lines.
Not so far reprinted.

A. 84 'Into her lying down head'

First appeared in *Life and Letters Today*, Vol. 27, No. 39, Nov. 1940, pp. 124–6.
First book form: *New Poems 1940*, New York, Yardstick Press, 1941.
Later in *N.P.*, pp. (2)–(4).
Later in *D.E.*, pp. 20–2, but with the last ten lines completely rewritten and four other small changes.
3 verses (numbered 'I'–'III') of 23 lines each.
C.P. pp. 113–15, same as *D.E.*

A. 85 'Deaths and Entrances'
('On almost the incendiary eve')

First appeared in *Horizon*, Vol. 3, No. 13, Jan. 1941, pp. 12–13.
First book form: *Poetry in Wartime*, London, Faber & Faber, 1942, pp. 169–70.

Later in *N.P.*, p. (23).

Later in *D.E.*, pp. 24–5, same as earlier printings except for *v.* 1, *l.* 3 which has here 'one at the great least' in place of 'one at the least'.

3 verses of 12 lines each.

C.P. pp. 117–18, same as *D.E.*

A. 86   'On a Wedding Anniversary'
                ('The sky is torn across')

First appeared in *Poetry* (London), No. 4, 15th Jan. 1941, p. 91, the first line being 'At last, in a wrong rain,' and the poem composed of:

4 verses of 5 lines each.

First book form: *Poetry in Wartime*, London, Faber & Faber, 1942, pp. 170–1.

Later in *N.P.*, pp. (10)–(11).

Later in *D.E.*, p. 32, but here several lines are rewritten, each verse is reduced by one line, one verse is dropped completely, and the verses appear in a different order. Roughly, verses 3, 4, and 1 of the early version form verses 1, 2, and 3 respectively of the later. *D.E.* has:

3 verses of 4 lines each.

C.P. p. 124, same as *D.E.*

Title remained unchanged through all printings.

A. 87   'Love in the Asylum'
                ('A stranger has come')

First appeared in *Poetry* (London), No. 6, May–June 1941, pp. 186–7.

First book form: *N.P.*, pp. (6)–(7).

Later in *D.E.*, p. 15, but here *v.* 2, *l.* 2 has 'mazed bed' in place of 'mad bed'.

6 verses of 3 lines each.

C.P. p. 108, same as *D.E.*

Same title in all printings.

A. 88   'Ballad of the Long-legged Bait'
                ('The bows glided down, and the coast')

First appeared in *Horizon*, Vol. 4, No. 19, July 1941, pp. 9–12.

First book form: *New Poems 1942*, Mount Vernon, N.Y., Peter Pauper Press, 1942.

Later in *N.P.*, pp. (13)–(20).

Later in *D.E.*, pp. 55–63, but here *v.* 15, *l.* 3 has 'rushing grave' in place of 'scuttled grave', *v.* 39 becomes italicized, and *v.* 44, *l.*3 has 'Time' in place of 'Times'.

54 verses of 4 lines each.

A facsimile of Thomas's work-sheet of verses 52 and 53 of this poem is reproduced in *Poets at Work*, New York, Harcourt Brace & Co., 1948, p. 164, showing earlier syntax and arrangement of these verses.

C.P. pp. 149–57, same as *D.E.* except for 'good-bye' and 'to-morrow' which appear each as one word in *D.E.* but are hyphenated in *C.P.* (various verses).

Same title in all printings.

A. 89   'Among those Killed in the Dawn Raid was a Man Aged a Hundred'
('When the morning was waking over the war')

First appeared in *Life and Letters Today*, Vol. 30, No. 48, Aug. 1941, p. 116.

First book form: *N.P.*, p. (5).

Later in *D.E.*, p. 41, but here *l.* 11 has 'spade's' in place of 'spades'' and there is no break.

L.L.T. and *N.P.*—2 verses of 8 and 6 lines.

D.E.—1 verse of 14 lines.

C.P. p. 135, same as *D.E.*

Same title in all printings.

A. 90   'The hunchback in the park'

First appeared in *Life and Letters Today*, Vol. 31, No. 50, Oct. 1941, pp. 41–2, first line as title.

First book form: *New Poems 1942*, Mount Vernon, N.Y., Peter Pauper Press, 1942.

Later in *N.P.*, pp. (9)–(10).

Later in *D.E.*, pp. 18–19, but with the following differences:

	L.L.T., etc.	*D.E.*
v. 1, *l.* 5	That let	That lets
v. 1, *l.* 6	dark,	dark
v. 5, *l.* 4	tiger	tigers
v. 6, *l.* 6	lock	locks

D

In addition, *L.L.T.* has lines 4 and 5 of *v.* 7 in the wrong order, and this is corrected in *D.E.*

7 verses of 6 lines each.

C.P. pp. 111–12, same as *D.E.*

This poem also occurs in 'Reminiscences of Childhood' (see C. 143), which, in its reprinted state in *Quite Early One Morning*, has a comma at the end of *l.* 6, *v.* 5 (the first impression even had a full stop, but this was subsequently modified).   *C.P.* has no punctuation here at all, maintaining the style of earlier printings.

A. 91   'On the Marriage of a Virgin'
('Waking alone in a multitude of loves when morning's light')

First appeared in *Life and Letters Today*, Vol. 31, No. 50, Oct. 1941, pp. 42–3, entitled 'The Marriage of a Virgin.'

First book form: *New Poems 1942*, Mount Vernon, N.Y., Peter Pauper Press, 1942.

Later in *N.P.*, p. (7).

Later in *D.E.*, p. 35, same as earlier printings but entitled 'On the Marriage of a Virgin.'

2 verses of 7 lines each.

C.P. p. 127, same as *D.E.*

A. 92   'Request to Leda'
('Not your winged lust but his must now change suit')
(Sub-titled 'Homage to William Empson.')

First appeared in *Horizon*, Vol. 6, No. 31, July 1942, p. 6.

First book form: *N.P.*, p. (22).

3 verses of 3 lines each.

Not in *D.E.* or *C.P.*

A. 93   'Ceremony After a Fire Raid'
('Myselves | The grievers | Grieve |' . . . etc.).

First appeared in *Our Time*, Vol. 3, No. 10, May 1944, p. 10.   (The centre pages, pp. 10–11, formed a special May Day poetry supplement dedicated to the memory of F. Garcia Lorca.)

First book form: *The War Poets*, New York, The John Day Co., 1945, pp. 433–5, but with Part I, *v.* 3 reduced by one line, and the one verse of Part III reduced by one line; there are also a few other minor changes as follows:

	Our Time	The War Poets
Pt. I, v. 4, l. 4	fire dwarfed	fire-dwarfed
Pt. II, v. 1, l. 9	bridegroom	bride groom
Pt. II, v. 2, l. 10	Nightfall. . . .	Night fall. . . .
	. . . the sun	. . . a sun
Pt. II, v. 2, l. 12	kindled	crumbled
Pt. III, l. 1	organ pipes	organpipes

The poem is in 3 parts numbered 'I'–'III,' which are composed as follows:

Our Time—Pt. I, 4 verses of 8 lines each; Pt. II, 2 verses of 14 lines each; Pt. III, 1 verse of 18 lines.

The War Poets—Pt. I, 4 verses of 8, 8, 7, and 8 lines; Pt. II, 2 verses of 14 lines each; Pt. III, 1 verse of 17 lines.

Later in *D.E.*, pp. 37–9, same as *The War Poets*.

C.P. pp. 129–31, same as *D.E.*

A. 94   'Last night I dived my beggar arm'

First appeared in *Poetry* (London), No. 9 (1944, probably June), p. 34, untitled.

2 verses of 4 lines each.   (The full stop at *l.* 4, *v.* 1 is obviously a misprint.)

First book form: *First Time in America: A Selection of Poems Never Before Published in the U.S.A.*, New York, Duell, Sloane & Pearce, 1948.

Not in *D.E.* or *C.P.*

Reprinted in *Poetry London–New York*, Vol. 1, No. 1, Mar.–Apr. 1956, p. 12, with the full stop at *l.* 4, *v.* 1 deleted and 'betrayal' corrected to 'betrayed' at *l.* 3, *v.* 2.

A. 95   'Your breath was shed'

First appeared in *Poetry* (London), No. 9 (1944—see A. 93), p. 34, entitled 'Poem.'

3 verses of 4 lines each.

First book form: *First Time in America: A Selection of Poems Never Before Published in the U.S.A.*, New York, Duell, Sloane & Pearce, 1948.

Not in *D.E.* or *C.P.*

A. 96   'Vision and Prayer'
('Who | are you | who is born | ' . . . etc.).

First appeared in *Horizon*, Vol. 11, No. 61, Jan. 1945, pp. 8–13.
First book form: *D.E.*, pp. 43–54, with the following differences:

	Horizon	*D.E.*
Pt. I, v. 4, l. 6	was lost who am	lost was who am
Pt. I, v. 4, l. 7	man-drenched	man drenched
Pt. I, v. 5, l. 6	judge-blown	judge blown
Pt. II, v. 3, l. 1	That he let	Then he let
Pt. II, v. 3, l. 14	Unsummoned by	Unbidden by

In 2 parts numbered 'I' and 'II,' consisting:
Pt. I: 6 verses of 17, 17, 17, 17, 16, and 17 lines.
Pt. II: 6 verses of 17, 17, 17, 17, 18, and 17 lines.
    C.P. pp. 43–54, same as *D.E.* but with the first and fourth differences above (probably both misprints) corrected to the original *Horizon* style.

A. 97   'Holy Spring'
('O | out of a bed of love | ' . . . etc.).

First appeared in *Horizon*, Vol. 11, No. 61, Jan. 1945, p. 14.
First book form: *The War Poets*, New York, The John Day Co., 1945, pp. 432–3.
Later in *D.E.*, p. 64, with two minor differences:

	Horizon	*D.E.*
v. 1, l. 6	assured an army	assumed an army
v. 1, l. 10	there are none	there is none

The first of these is obviously a misprint and is corrected in *The War Poets* as well as *D.E.*
2 verses of 12 lines each.
C.P. p. 158, same as *D.E.*

A. 98   'Poem in October'
('It was my thirtieth year to heaven')

First appeared in *Horizon*, Vol. 11, No. 62, Feb. 1945, pp. 82–3.
First book form: *D.E.*, pp. 9–11, with several punctuation variations as follows:

Drawing by Brenda Chamberlain for
FROM IN MEMORY OF ANN JONES (B. 8)

	Horizon	*D.E.*
v. 1, l. 7	net-webbed	net webbed
v. 4, l. 2	sea-wet	sea wet
v. 4, l 4,	owls,	owls
v. 4, l. 7	lark-full	lark full
v. 5, l. 1	country,	country
v. 5, l. 5	currants,	currants
v. 6, l. 10	singing birds	singingbirds
v. 7, l. 3	long-dead	long dead

D.E. was published in Feb. 1946.   Nine months after this, however, the earlier version of this poem appeared in book form, in *Little Reviews Anthology 1946*, London, Eyre & Spottiswoode, 1946, pp. 89–91, and in July 1947 (though dated 1946) yet again in *Poetry Since 1939*, London, Longmans Green & Co. Ltd. (published for The British Council) pp. 45–7.

7 verses of 10 lines each.

This was one of Thomas's own favourite poems; he recorded it for the collection of records known as *Pleasure Dome*, Columbia Records Inc., 1948, and it has been reprinted many times in English and also in German and Danish.

C.P. pp. 102–4, same as *D.E.*

A. 99   'A Refusal to Mourn the Death, by Fire, of a Child in London'
('Never until the mankind making')

First appeared in the *New Republic*, Vol. 112, No. 20, 14th May 1945 (No. 1589), p. 675.

First book form: *War and the Poet*, New York, The Devin-Adair Co., 1945 (Oct.), pp. 200–1.

Later in *D.E.*, p. 8.

4 verses of 6 lines each.

C.P. p. 101.

All printings of this poem as detailed above are identical.

A. 100   'Lie still, sleep becalmed, sufferer with the wound'

First appeared in *Life and Letters Today*, Vol. 45, No. 94, June 1945, p. 155, entitled 'Lie Still, Sleep Becalmed.'

First book form: *D.E.*, p. 42.

3 verses of 4, 4, and 6 lines.

C.P. p. 136.

All the above printings are identical.

A. 101   'This Side of the Truth (for Llewelyn)'
('This side of the truth,')

First appeared in *Life and Letters Today*, Vol. 46, No. 95, July 1945, pp. 28–9.

Appeared three or four days later in *The New Republic*, Vol. 113, No. 1, 2nd July 1945 (No. 1596), p. 20.

First book form: *D.E.*, pp. 12–13.

3 verses of 12 lines each.

C.P. pp. 105–6.

All the above printings are identical.

A. 102   'The Conversation of Prayer'
('The conversation of prayers about to be said')

The first version of this poem, published in America, constitutes the second printing. Doubtless Thomas sent it to the periodical in question some weeks earlier than that which appeared in London, and in the meantime made an alteration. The first version appeared in the *New Republic*, Vol. 113, No. 3, 16th July 1945 (No. 1598), p. 76, where the end of *l*. 3, *v*. 4 reads '. . . deep as his made grave,'. Title: 'The Conversation of Prayers.'

First appearance, however, was in *Life and Letters Today*, Vol. 46, No. 95, July 1945, p. 29, with *l*. 3, *v*. 4 reading '. . . deep as his true grave,'.

First book form: *D.E.*, p. 7, same as *L.L.T.* but entitled 'The Conversation of Prayer' and with the correction 'Whom', *v*. 3, *l*. 1, in place of 'Who'.

4 verses of 5 lines each.

C.P. p. 100, same as *D.E.* but with 'To-night', *v*. 3, *l*. 5, in place of 'To night'.

A. 103   'A Winter's Tale'
('It is a winter's tale')

First appeared in *Poetry* (Chicago), Vol. 66, July 1945, pp. 175–80.
First book form: *D.E.*, pp. 26–31, with the following differences:

	Poetry	D.E.
v. 7, l. 2	made sky	veiled sky
v. 7, l. 4	styes	sties
v. 20, l. 1	knee	knee-
v. 20, l. 3	she	she-
v. 26, l. 2	whirl	whirl-

26 verses of 5 lines each.

C.P. pp. 119–23, same as *D.E.* but with 'milkmaids', *v.* 5, *l.* 3, in place of 'milk maids'.

A. 104   'Fern Hill'
('Now as I was young and easy under the apple boughs')

First appeared in *Horizon*, Vol. 12, No. 70, Oct. 1945, pp. (221)–222.
First book form: *D.E.*, pp. 65–6, with the following minor differences.

	Horizon	*D.E.*
v. 3, *l.* 1	hay-	hay
v. 4, *l.* 2	shoulder:	shoulder;
v. 5, *l.* 5	house-high	house high

6 verses of 9 lines each.
This poem has been much reprinted and has appeared translated in German and Danish periodicals.

C.P. pp. 159–61, same as *D.E.* but with the colon after 'shoulder', *v.* 4, *l.* 2, as originally.

A. 105   'In my craft or sullen art'

First appeared in *Life and Letters Today*, Vol. 47, No. 98, Oct. 1945, p. 31, first line as title.
1 verse of 20 lines.
First book form: *D.E.*, p. 36, same as *L.L.T.* but with a break after line 11 making:
2 verses of 11 and 9 lines.
Recorded by Thomas in *Pleasure Dome*, Columbia Records Inc., 1948.
C.P. p. 128, same as *D.E.*

A. 106   'In Country Sleep'
('Never and never, my girl riding far and near')

First appeared in *Horizon*, Vol. 16, No. 96, Dec. 1947, pp. 302–5, but with 11 (mostly obvious) misprints.
First book form: *Little Reviews Anthology 1949*, London, Methuen, 1949, pp. 68–71, same as *Horizon* (i.e. with the same misprints).

Later in *26 P.*, pp. 72–6, with the misprints corrected and with the following other alterations:

	Horizon	26 P.
Pt. I, v. 2, l. 1	ever	ever,
Pt. I, v. 3, l. 7	stern.	stern
Pt. I, v. 4, l. 3	caverned	ravened
Pt. I, v. 5, l. 7	Fear mask	Fear most
Pt. I, v. 6, l. 3	Jew	dew
Pt. I, v. 7, l. 7	Be sure	Be you sure
Pt. I, v. 8, l. 3	the sleep	to sleep
Pt. I, v. 8, l. 4	last love	lost love
Pt. I, v. 9, l. 1	the snow	the fleece
Pt. I, v. 9, l. 5	Appleseed	Apple seed
Pt. I, v. 9, l. 6	wounds	wound
Pt. II, v. 2, l. 1	grape green wrist	winged, sloe wrist
Pt. II, v. 7, l. 6	loosed, dumb	lawless
Pt. II, v. 8, l. 5	reach first	and each first

Later in *In Country Sleep*, New York, 1952, pp. 28–34, same as *26 P.*

In 2 parts, numbered 'I' and 'II.' Part I, 9 verses of 7 lines each; Part II, 8 verses of 6 lines each.

C.P. pp. 162–6, same as *26 P.* but with 'black-backed' in place of 'black backed', Part II, v. 4, l. 1, and 'willy nilly' in place of 'willynilly', Part II, v. 5, l. 6.

A. 107   'Over Sir John's hill,'

First appeared in *Botteghe Oscure*, No. 4, Rome, 1949, pp. 397–9, first line as title.

First book form: *A Little Treasury of British Poetry: The Chief Poets from 1500 to 1950*, New York, Charles Scribner's Sons, 1951.

Later in *In Country Sleep*, New York, 1952, pp. 9–12.

5 verses of 12 lines each.

C.P. pp. 167–9, same as *I.C.S.* except for the following differences:

	I.C.S.	C.P.
v. 3, l. 1	And hear	And read
v. 3, l. 3	hawk eyed	hawk-eyed
v. 3, l. 12	the distant	the shell-hung distant

A. 108   'In the White Giant's Thigh'
('Through throats where many rivers meet, the curlews cry,')

First appeared in *Botteghe Oscure*, No. 6, Rome, Nov. 1950, pp. 335–7, followed by a note on the poem by the author (pp. 337–8).

First book form: *A Little Treasury of British Poetry : The Chief Poets from 1500 to 1950*, New York, Charles Scribner's Sons, 1951.

Later in *I.C.S.*, pp. 23-7, but with spacing rearranged and the last 12 lines rewritten.

60 lines, grouped not in 'verses' in the strict sense but freely according to the pulse of the poem.   That Thomas did not build the poem round a rigid preconceived framework is indicated by the rearrangement in the second version.

The original note on this poem, in *Botteghe Oscure*, states that it is part of a long poem—'In Country Heaven'—in preparation.

C.P. pp. 176-8, same as *I.C.S.* but with 'harvest kneels' in place of 'harvest bows', *l.* 50.

A. 109   'Do not go gentle into that good night,'

First appeared in *Botteghe Oscure*, No. 8, Rome, Nov. 1951, p. 208, first line as title.

First book form: *I.C.S.*, pp. 18-19, same as *Botteghe Oscure* but with 'crying', *v.* 3, *l.* 1, in place of 'sighing'.

6 verses of 3, 3, 3, 3, 3, and 4 lines.

C.P. p. 116, same as *I.C.S.*   (Proof copies of *C.P.* have 'Paper and Sticks'—excluded from the published edition—on this page.)

A. 110   'Lament'
('When I was a windy boy and a bit')

First appeared in *Botteghe Oscure*, No. 8, Rome, Nov. 1951, pp. 209-10.

First book form: *I.C.S.*, pp. 20-2, but with various revisions and an additional verse.

Botteghe Oscure—4 verses of 12 lines each.

I.C.S.—5 verses of 12 lines each.

C.P. pp. 174-5, same as *I.C.S.*

A. 111   'Poem on His Birthday.'
('In the mustardseed sun,')

First appeared in *World Review*, New Series, No. 32, Oct. 1951, pp. 66-7.

First book form: *I.C.S.*, pp. 13-17, with various revisions and 3 additional verses.

World Review—9 verses of 9 lines each.

I.C.S.—12 verses of 9 lines each.

C.P. pp. 170-3, same as *I.C.S.*

A. 112   'Prologue'
             ('This day winding down now')

First appeared in the *Listener*, Vol. 48, No. 1236, 6th Nov. 1952, p. 773 (from a broadcast, in which the poem was read by the author, on 26th Oct. 1952).

First book form: (4 days later) *C.P.*, pp. vii–x, same as the *Lis.*, but entitled 'Author's Prologue'.

This poem, written specially for *C.P.*, is in 2 verses of 51 lines each, each verse rhyming backwards with the other, i.e. line 1 with line 102, 2 with 101, etc.

(*See plate opposite.*)

A. 113   Elegy
             ('Too proud to die, broken and blind he died')

This poem—as far as is known, his last—remained unfinished at the time of Thomas's death.   First printed mention of it occurs in the *Fifth Annual Report to the Fellows of the Pierpont Morgan Library*, New York, Nov. 1954, within a note, pp. 57–8, explaining how a draft of eight lines of the poem came to be presented to the Library by Mr Ruthven Todd.   The draft (which was in fact the first of many) is referred to as an 'eight verse stanza'—a misprint for 'eight line stanza.' The note refers to the poem as concerning the death of the poet's father, and quotes the opening two and a half lines as follows:

> 'A cold, kind man brave in his narrow pride,
> Too proud to die, broken and blind he died
> The darkest way . . .'

Thomas gave the MS. of this draft to Mr Todd on 3rd Nov. 1953—the day before his sudden final collapse.

The next printed evidence of this poem, showing a further development, appeared in *Dylan Thomas in America*, by John Malcolm Brinnin (Boston, Little, Brown & Co, 1955), pp. 227–8, where eight lines—almost identical to the first eight of the final version—are quoted. Here the first line reads: 'Too proud to die, broken and blind he died'.

The poem appeared *in toto* in *Encounter*, No. 29 (Vol. 6, No. 2), Feb. 1956, pp. 30–1, entitled 'Elegy,' extended and built up by the poet's friend, Vernon Watkins, from the sixty pages of MS. work Thomas left towards it, to a total length of forty lines.   Mr Watkins's note, which follows the poem (p. 31), explains how he developed and completed the poem from Thomas's preliminary drafts.

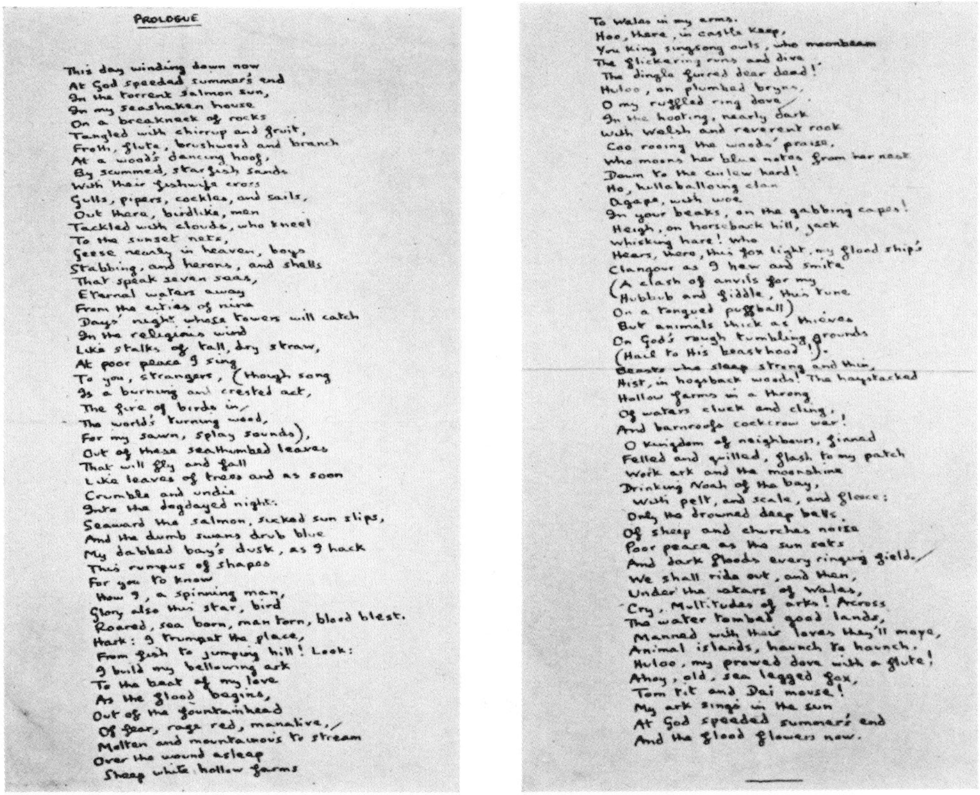

PROLOGUE

This day winding down now
At God speeded summer's end
In the torrent salmon sun,
In my seashaken house
On a breakneck of rocks
Tangled with chirrup and fruit,
Froth, flute, brushwood and branch
At a wood's dancing hoof,
By scummed, starfish sands
With their fishwife cross
Gulls, pipers, cockles, and sails,
Out there, birdlike, men
Tackled with clouds, who kneel
To the sunset nets,
Geese nearly in heaven, boys
Stabbing, and herons, and shells
That speak seven seas,
Eternal waters away
From the cities of nine
Days' night whose towers will catch
In the religious wind
Like stalks of tall, dry straw,
At poor peace I sing
To you, strangers, (though song
Is a burning and crested act,
The fire of birds in
The world's turning wood,
For my sawn, splay sounds),
Out of these seathumbed leaves
That will fly and fall
Like leaves of trees and as soon
Crumble and undie
Into the dogdayed night.
Seaward the salmon, sucked sun slips,
And the dumb swans drub blue
My dabbed bay's dusk, as I hack
This rumpus of shapes
For you to know
How I, a spinning man,
Glory also this star, bird
Roared, sea born, man torn, blood blest.
Hark: I trumpet the place,
From fish to jumping hill! Look:
I build my bellowing ark
To the best of my love
As the flood begins,
Out of the fountainhead
Of fear, rage red, manalive,
Molten and mountainous to stream
Over the wound asleep
Sheep white hollow farms

To Wales in my arms.
Hoo, there, in castle keep,
You king singsong owls, who moonbeam
The flickering runs and dive
The dingle furred deer dead!
Huloo, on plumbed bryns,
O my ruffled ring dove
In the hooting, nearly dark
With Welsh and reverent rook
Coo rooing the woods' praise,
Who moons her blue notes from her nest
Down to the curlew herd!
Ho, hullaballoing clan
Agape, with woe
In your beaks, on the gabbing capes!
Heigh, on horseback hill, jack
Whisking hare! who
Hears, there, this fox light, my flood ship's
Clangour as I hew and smite
(A clash of anvils for my
Hubbub and fiddle, this tune
On a tongued puffball)
But animals thick as thieves
On God's rough tumbling grounds
(Hail to His beasthood!).
Beasts who sleep strong and thin,
Hist, in hogsback woods! The haystacked
Hollow farms in a throng
Of waters cluck and cling,
And barnroofs cockcrow war!
O kingdom of neighbours, finned
Felled and quilled, flash to my patch
Work ark and the moonshine
Drinking Noah of the bay,
With pelt, and scale, and fleece:
Only the drowned deep bells
Of sheep and churches noise
Poor peace as the sun sets
And dark floods every ringing field.
We shall ride out, and then,
Under the stars of Wales,
Cry, Multitudes of arks! Across
The water tombed good lands,
Manned with their loves they'll move,
Animal islands, haunch to haunch.
Huloo, my prowed dove with a flute!
Ahoy, old, sea legged fox,
Tom tit and Dai mouse!
My ark sings in the sun
At God speeded summer's end
And the flood flowers now.

'Prologue' to COLLECTED POEMS—original MS., reduced (A. 112)

Section B

Books and Pamphlets by Dylan Thomas

Note

EXCEPT in the case of *18 Poems*, details of leaf gatherings are not given in this section since there does not seem, in any impression of any book, any good reason for this information.

Printing numbers of the American trade editions are approximate in that no hard and fast figure was demanded of the binders and often the quantity supplied by them fell short of or exceeded slightly the figure here mentioned.

Proof copies are not mentioned except where some special significance attaches to them, but they may be taken to exist in the case of all bound books (trade editions) except *18 Poems*. The quantity of such proofs can be reckoned at about thirty copies before and during the war and about double this figure or even slightly more thereafter.

Any notes of interest on contents of books rather than their physical appearance are appended in all cases to the descriptions of the first editions.

In 1938, reference was made in certain literary periodicals and elsewhere to a 'forthcoming' book of stories by Dylan Thomas entitled *The Burning Baby*—one magazine actually announced a review of the book as appearing in their next issue. The book was to have been published by Mr George Reavey's 'Europa Press,' after having been rejected in MS. by a number of other publishers, and was to have included the following stories:

The Orchards—The Enemies—The Mouse and the Woman—The Dress—The School for Witches—The Map of Love—The Horse's Ha—The Roundabouts (almost certainly the story now known as 'After the Fair')—The Lemon—The True Story—The Tree—The [*sic*] Prospect of the Sea—The Burning Baby—Prologue to an Adventure—The Holy Six—The Visitor.

For various reasons, however, not the least of which was the uneasiness of the international situation, plans for the publication of this book were frustrated and the MS. placed in other hands. Correspondence shortly after this (Mar. 1939) refers to some of the stories as being scheduled to appear in a book to have been entitled *In the*

Direction of the Beginning—probably a proposed title for what was to be, a few months later, *The Map of Love.*

Whatever the above may suggest, collectors may rest assured that *The Burning Baby*, as a book, does not, in fact, exist—even in proof, the only printed material extant being a few specimen pages set up by the intended printers in various types for the consideration of the Europa Press.

Order throughout this section is chronological except for item B. 2 (*18 Poems.* Fortune Press edition); the description of this item refers considerably to item B. 1 and I have felt that in this case system must give way to convenience.

B. 1   1 8 POEMS (First edition)

(*a*) *First Issue.*

18 | POEMS | DYLAN   THOMAS | (space) | Published   by | THE SUNDAY REFEREE and | THE PARTON BOOKSHOP | PARTON STREET, LONDON, W.C.1.

Demy 8vo ($8\frac{5}{8}'' \times 5\frac{3}{8}''$), black cloth, spine lettered in gold ('18 POEMS by DYLAN THOMAS') from just below centre reading upwards; flat spine; top edge cut, fore and bottom edges roughly trimmed; end-papers white; issued in a pale grey dust-wrapper lettered in a darker grey.

Collation: 36 + (4) pp. consisting of one gathering of four leaves unsigned, and two gatherings of eight leaves signed B and C at pp. 9 and 25, made up as follows: (1)–(2) half-title, verso blank; (3)–(4) title, verso 'First published 1934 | (space) | Made and printed in Great Britain by | THE FAVIL PRESS, LTD. | 152 CHURCH STREET | LONDON, W.8.'; (5)–(6) 'This book, the second volume of the Sunday Referee Poets | series, is unaccompanied by either portrait or preface, at | the author's request. | VICTOR S. NEUBURG | Poetry Editor, *Sunday Referee.* | (space) | (acknowledgments)', verso Contents; (7)–(8) contents continued, verso blank; 9–36 text of the poems; (37)–(38) blank leaf; (39)–(40) colophon, verso blank.

Publication. Five hundred sets of sheets were printed but in the first instance only two hundred and fifty were bound, made up as described above, and issued on or within a very few days of 18th Dec. 1934, at 3s. 6d.   A few review copies were sent out prior to this date. The first review of the book that I have been able to trace appeared in the *Morning Post* dated 1st Jan. 1935, p. 17, under the somewhat erroneous heading: 'Published Today.'   No proof copies were made up, the only proofs printed being the galley proofs.

(*See plate facing p. 41.*)

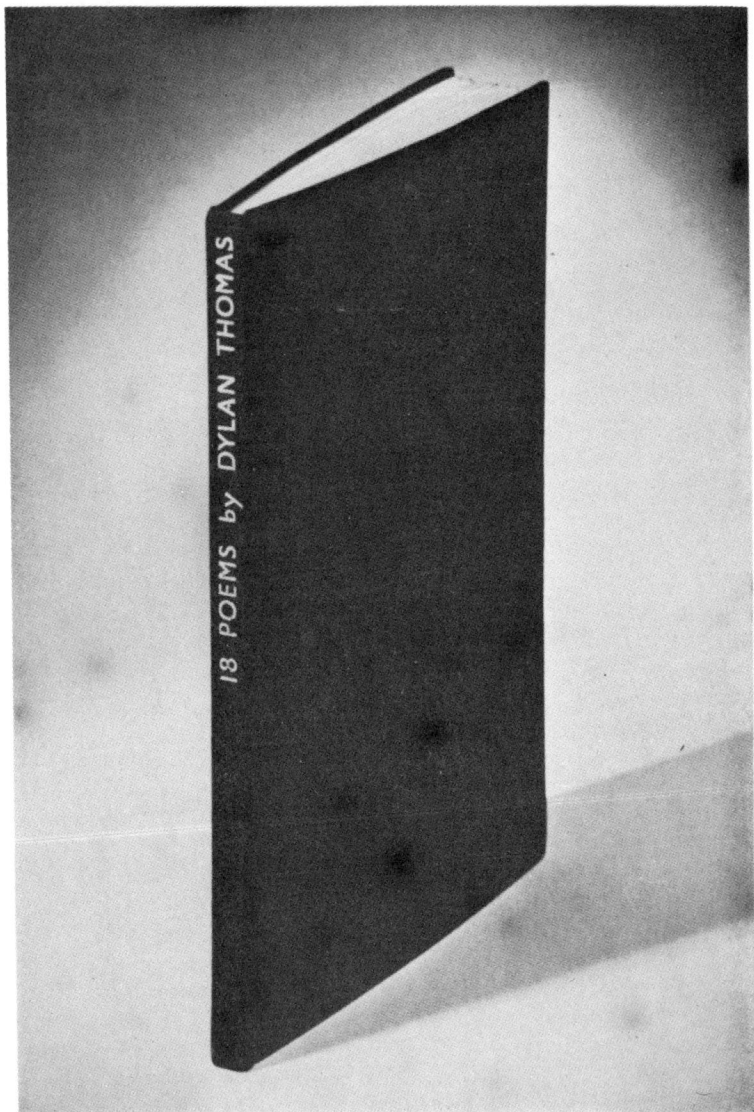

18 Poems—first issue binding (B. 1)

(b) *Second Issue.*

The remaining two hundred and fifty sets of sheets, constituting the second issue, were bound up about a year later and published on 21st Feb. 1936, again at 3s. 6d. (not 5s. as advertised).   (On the same day, and also from the Parton Bookshop, David Gascoyne's *Man's Life Is This Meat* was issued.)

This issue differed from the first as follows:

Round-backed spine; fore-edge cut, all leaves evenly; extra leaf tipped in between half-title and title, recto blank, verso advertising *Thirty Preliminary Poems* by George Barker, *18 Poems* by Dylan Thomas, and *Man's Life Is This Meat* by David Gascoyne; blocking on spine executed in Dutch gold, which becomes easily discoloured, as against the real gold of the first issue.

Other alleged points of issue should be regarded with caution. Although the paper of most second issue copies I have examined appears to be thicker and of somewhat poorer quality than that of the first, the paper on which the entire edition was printed was, as noted in the colophon, Glastonbury Antique Laid.   Neither can end-papers, whether wove or laid, be justifiably treated as indicating issue, since both types occur in each and it seems fairly certain that the end-papers were, throughout the edition, made up of 'ends' the printers had. On the other hand the flat spine of the first issue is not perhaps so arbitrary as it sounds or difficult to identify.   A tough flat strip of card, whose width corresponds exactly to the thickness of the book, is situated under the cloth and can be felt easily, whereas the later style incorporates a thinner and more flexible strip which is slightly wider and therefore must, of necessity, be rounded so as not to protrude beyond the covers. I have seen one copy of this book with the second issue sheets (including the advert leaf) in the first issue binding; there may well be others in this state but I should estimate their number to be extremely few.

History.   At the time when Thomas's poems first began to appear in it, in 1933, the *Sunday Referee* included a weekly 'Literary and Entertainment Supplement' of some twenty pages, of which 'Poet's Corner' (later renamed more correctly 'Poets' Corner') occupied rather less than a quarter of a page.   After Mar. 1934 the Supplement ceased as such, though many of its features, including 'Poets' Corner' until Nov. 1935, were transferred to the main body of the paper. The 'Corner' was edited, with the assistance of Runia Sheila MacLeod, by Victor Neuburg, who inaugurated a system of prizes which were awarded to the poet who had submitted a poem adjudged to have been the most outstanding of those printed over a period of six months. The prize itself consisted of the publication, under the aegis of the *Sunday Referee*, of a book of the winning poet's work.   The first of these prizes was awarded to Pamela Hansford Johnson in 1933.

In all, 'Poets' Corner' published seven poems by Thomas. The second of these, 'The force that through the green fuse drives the flower,' appeared on 29th Oct. 1933, and on 22nd Apr. 1934 it was announced that this poem had gained for him the second award of the Book Prize. *18 Poems* should have appeared not many weeks later, but the publishers in whose hands the MS. had been placed could not arrive at a decision as to its acceptance. On 10th June Neuburg stated that he hoped 'to make an announcement' about the book 'next week,' but by 7th Oct. the position was unchanged and further 'delay' was referred to. It was at this time that the MS. was withdrawn from the publishers originally approached and placed with Mr David Archer of the Parton Bookshop. It transpired that Archer had already read much of Thomas's work and appreciated its merit, and he at once made arrangements to have the book manufactured. Of the printing cost, Mr Mark Goulden of the *Sunday Referee* put up £30, and the balance—£20—was contributed by Archer.

Although *18 Poems* was Thomas's first book it does not constitute his first appearance in book form—*The Year's Poetry* (1934), containing the poem 'Light breaks where no sun shines,' having been published on 4th Dec. 1934. (*See* D. 1.)

Contents. The poems are untitled save for the numbers from 'One' to 'Eighteen' [*sic*]. First lines are: I see the boys of summer in their ruin—When once the twilight locks no longer—A process in the weather of the heart—Before I knocked and flesh let enter,—The force that through the green fuse drives the flower—My hero bares his nerves along my wrist—Where once the waters of your face—If I were tickled by the rub of love,—Our eunuch dreams, all seedless in the light,—Especially when the October wind—When, like a running grave, time tracks you down,—From love's first fever to her plague, from the soft second—In the beginning was the three-pointed star,—Light breaks where no sun shines;—I fellowed sleep who kissed me in the brain,—I dreamed my genesis in sweat of sleep, breaking—Half of the fellow father as he doubles—All all and all the dry worlds lever,.

B. 2   18 POEMS (Second edition)

18 | POEMS | by | DYLAN   THOMAS | (space) | THE   FORTUNE PRESS | 12 BUCKINGHAM PALACE ROAD | LONDON

Demy 8vo ($8\frac{3}{4}'' \times 5\frac{1}{2}''$), red buckram, spine blocked centrally with title and author's name in gold reading upwards; top edge cut, fore-edge uncut, bottom edge unevenly trimmed; end-papers white; issued in a yellow dust-wrapper lettered in red.

Collation: 32 pp. consisting: (1)–(2) title, verso 'First published in 1934 . . .'; (3)–(4) Contents, verso continued; 5–(32) text of the poems.

Publication. No records are available as to the number of copies first issued or date of publication, but the fact that Fortune Press advertisements do not include this book until 1942 would seem to indicate the approximate date. The B.M. copy was received on 7th July 1942. The price was 6*s*.

There have been many issues of this book, of which the first was as described above. Later issues have varying cloths and colours, one issue having boards and a cloth back.

Contents. As B. 1, the versions of the poems themselves being identical (issues after the publication of *Collected Poems* to date retaining the original versions).

B. 3   TWENTY-FIVE POEMS

TWENTY-FIVE POEMS | DYLAN THOMAS | (space) | LONDON: J. M. DENT & SONS LTD.

Crown 8vo ($7\frac{1}{4}''$ × $5\frac{3}{8}''$).   Grey boards, spine lettered downwards in dark blue.   All edges cut.   There are no end-papers, but, of the four eight-leaf gatherings, (A)1 and D8 are pasted down.   Grey dust-wrapper lettered in blue and black.

Collation: 1 blank leaf; (i)–(ii) half-title, verso listing uniform volumes in the series; (iii)–(iv) title, verso ' . . . First published 1936'; v–vi Contents (recto and verso); vii–viii Acknowledgments and a two-line note on the last poem in the book, verso blank; 1–47 text of the poems; (48) Temple Press device; one blank leaf.

Publication. Published on 10th Sept. 1936, at 2*s*. 6*d*., as the fifteenth volume of a 'New Poetry' series in uniform format.   Seven hundred and thirty copies were printed of the first impression.   Subsequent impressions, of which there were three, are identifiable by a note of the fact on the verso of the title-page, and since each 'issue' constituted a separate impression there are no 'issue points.'

History. After the variously toned but never indifferent reception accorded to *18 Poems*, Thomas's name began to appear regularly in a number of literary journals.   But Victor Neuburg felt that the opportunities provided by that book and the auguries of 'promise' which it had elicited from the critics should not be left too long in mid air, and early in 1936 he suggested that Thomas might collect together what poems he had written over the past year with a view to preparing a second book.   Within a few days Thomas had handed him a sheaf of twenty-one poems. Neuburg, having read and been impressed by them, advised making up the number to a round twenty-five. The additional four were quickly supplied and, whilst it is unlikely that they were specially written for the book, it may be worth noting that the seven poems whose original placings I have been unable to trace all appeared for the first time in book form in *Twenty-Five Poems*, and it would therefore seem probable that these four last-minute additions, at least, had not in fact previously been published.

Contents. The poems are untitled and unnumbered but are listed in the Contents—including each of the ten sonnets (numbered i–x) which form the twenty-fifth poem—by their first lines as follows: I, in my intricate image, stride on two levels—This bread I break was once the oat—Incarnate devil in a talking snake—Today, this insect, and the world I breathe—The seed-at-zero shall not storm—Shall gods be said to thump the clouds—Here in this spring, stars float along the void—Do you not father me, nor the erected arm—Out of the sighs a little comes—Hold hard, these ancient minutes in the cuckoo's month —Was there a time when dancers with their fiddles—Now (|say nay,| etc.)—Why east wind chills and south wind cools—A grief ago—How soon the servant sun—Ears in the turrets hear—Foster the light nor veil the manshaped moon—The hand that signed the paper felled a city— Should lanterns shine, the holy face—I have longed to move away— Find meat on bones that soon have none—Grief thief of time crawls off—And death shall have no dominion—Then was my neophyte— (Sonnet sequence:) (i) Altarwise by owl-light in the halfway-house— (ii) Death is all metaphors, shape in one history—(iii) First there was the lamb on knocking knees—(iv) What is the metre of the dictionary? —(v) And from the windy West came two-gunned Gabriel—(vi) Cartoon of slashes on the tide-traced crater—(vii) Now stamp the Lord's Prayer on a grain of rice—(viii) This was the crucifixion on the mountain—(ix) From the oracular archives and the parchment— (x) Let the tale's sailor from a Christian Voyage.

(*See plate facing p. 80.*)

B. 4   THE MAP OF LOVE

The Map of Love | VERSE AND PROSE | by | Dylan Thomas | (space) | LONDON | J. M. DENT & SONS LTD.

(*a*) *First Issue.*
Demy 8vo ($8\frac{3}{8}'' \times 5\frac{1}{4}''$), issued in a fine-grained mauve cloth with title blocked in gold on upper part of front cover; spine blocked horizontally with title and author's name in gold on upper half, 'Dent' blind at foot; all edges cut; top edge stained dark purple; front end-papers only

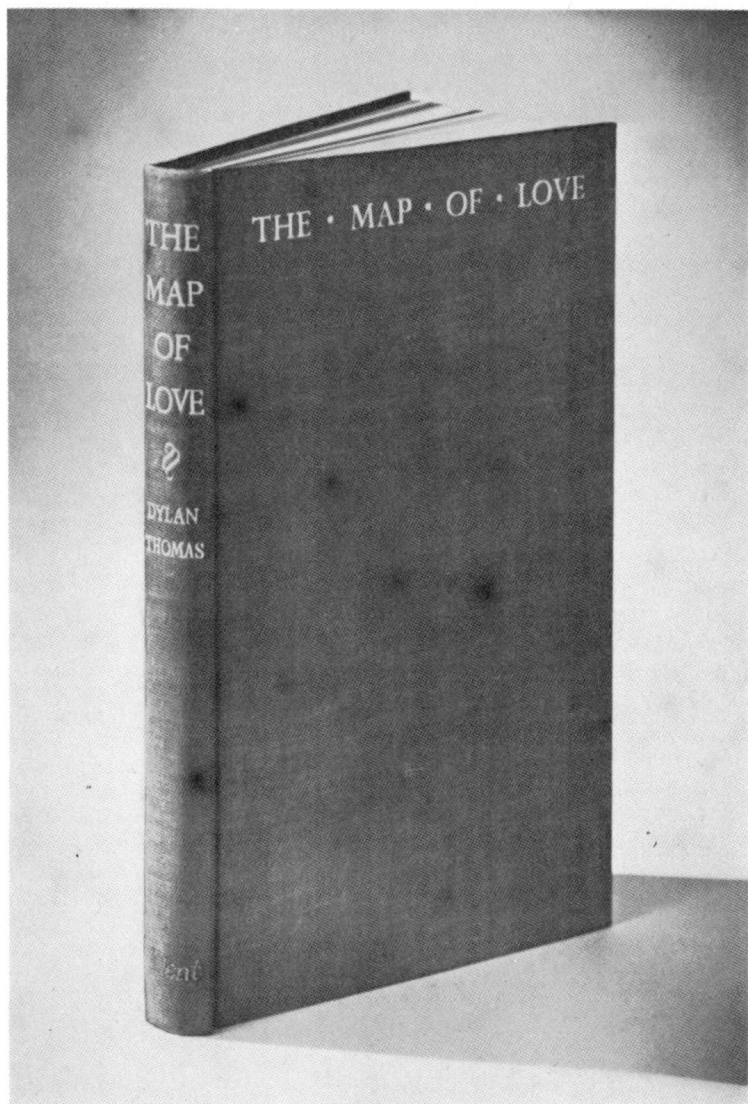

THE MAP OF LOVE—first issue binding (B. 4)

(white), H8 at end being a paste-down; issued in a grey and purple dust-wrapper.

Collation: (i)–(ii) half-title, verso 'BY THE SAME AUTHOR | TWENTY-FIVE POEMS'; tipped in frontis., recto blank, verso portrait of Thomas by Augustus John; (iii)–(iv) title, verso ' . . . First Published 1939'; (v)–(vi) dedication 'To Caitlin,' verso blank; vii–viii Contents (recto 'Verse', verso 'Prose'); (1)–(2) section heading ('Verse') verso blank; 3–24 text of the poems; (25)–(26) section heading ('Prose'), verso blank; 27–(116) text of the prose; one blank leaf.

Publication. 2,000 sets of sheets were printed in 1939 and no further impression was made. Of these the first issue, as described above, consisted of 1,000 copies on 24th Aug. 1939. Published price 7s. 6d.

(*See plate facing p. 44.*)

(*b*) *Second Issue.*
On 8th Apr. 1947—consisted of 250 copies, bound in a coarser and plum-coloured cloth but otherwise same as first issue.

(*c*) *Third Issue.*
In Feb. 1948—consisted of 250 copies, bound in purple cloth (texture roughly midway between that of the first and second issues), blocked entirely in blue—i.e. including 'Dent' at foot of spine. In other respects same as first issue.

(*d*) *Fourth Issue.*
Between Dec. 1948 and Feb. 1949—consisted of the remaining 500 copies, bound exactly as the *third* issue but with the top edge unstained.

The three shades of cloth are easily distinguishable; as a guide to each the following amplifications may assist:
The first style was a pure mauve and of an almost silky texture; the second was a rather deep, almost 'Victoria,' plum, somewhat loosely woven; the third and fourth (each in the same cloth) were not quite the deep 'regal' shade of purple, and the cloth itself, though as tightly woven, was of rather thicker strands than that of the first. The third and fourth issues are, however, most readily recognized by the blue lettering, the plain or stained top edge distinguishing the one from the other.

Contents. The poems are numbered, 1–16, but are otherwise untitled save for 'After the funeral . . . ' which is headed ' (In memory of Ann Jones).' Contents table lists the poems by their first lines and

E

the prose pieces by their titles, as follows: (Verse): Because the
pleasure-bird whistles after the hot wires—I make this in a warring
absence when—When all my five and country senses see—We lying by
seasand, watching yellow—It is the sinners' dust-tongued bell claps
me to churches—O make me a mask and a wall to shut from your spies—
The spire cranes. Its statue is an aviary—After the funeral, mule
praises, brays—Once it was the colour of saying—Not from this anger,
anticlimax after—How shall my animal—The tombstone told when she
died—On no work of words now for three lean months in the bloody—
A saint about to fall—If my head hurt a hair's foot—Twenty-four years
remind the tears of my eyes. (Prose) The Visitor—The Enemies—
The Tree—The Map of Love—The Mouse and the Woman—The Dress
—The Orchards.

All the prose pieces commence on right-hand pages, and as two of
them also end thus pp. 72 and 102 are blank.

The same prose works appeared in *The World I Breathe* (with the
exception of 'The Tree') a year later, and in 1955 in *Adventures in the
Skin Trade* and *A Prospect of the Sea*.

The entire contents of *The Map of Love* had earlier appeared in periodicals (*see* Section C).

B. 5   THE WORLD I BREATHE

THE WORLD I BREATHE | DYLAN THOMAS (name in brown,
within black ornamental enclosure) | NEW DIRECTIONS ·
NORFOLK · CONN.

Medium 8vo (9⅛" × 6¼"), light brown buckram, spine blocked in
gold from head to foot as follows: ' * * * * * DYLAN THOMAS
* * * * * '; top and bottom edges cut, shallow-trimmed fore-edge;
end-papers deep cream (same as leaves); issued in a cream dust-wrapper
lettered in blue and brown.

Collation: 183 pp. consisting: one blank leaf; (i)–(ii) title, verso
'copyright 1939, new directions'; (1)–(2) Contents, verso Contents
(contd.); (3)–(4) Contents (contd.), verso blank; (5)–(6) 'POEMS,'
verso blank; 7–77 text of the poems; (78) blank; (79)–(80)
'STORIES,' verso blank; 81–183 text of the stories; (184) colophon
'(device) | seven hundred copies printed for | new directions | at
the walpole printing office | november 1939'; two blank leaves.

Publication. 700 copies were published on 20th Dec. 1939, at
$2.50. There was no further issue.

Contents. 40 poems, selected from *18 Poems*, *Twenty-Five Poems*, and
The Map of Love (the sonnet sequence from *Twenty-Five Poems* treated as

one poem) and the following stories: The Dress—The Visitor—The Map of Love—The Enemies—The Orchards—The Mouse and the Woman—The Holy Six—A Prospect of the Sea—The Burning Baby—Prologue to an Adventure—The School for Witches.

Of the stories, the first six are from *The Map of Love*, 'The Burning Baby' and 'The School for Witches' first appeared in book form in *New Directions 1939* (D. 7), and 'The Holy Six,' 'A Prospect of the Sea,' and 'Prologue to an Adventure' here appear in book form for the first time.

The World I Breathe is perhaps, at least in Great Britain, the most scarce of Thomas's books. The title is derived from the poem commencing 'Today, this insect, and the world I breathe' in *Twenty-Five Poems* and included in this volume.

B. 6　PORTRAIT OF THE ARTIST AS A YOUNG DOG

First (English) edition.
Portrait of the Artist | as a Young Dog | BY DYLAN THOMAS | (space) | DENT · LONDON

Crown 8vo ($7\frac{1}{4}'' \times 4\frac{3}{4}''$), green cloth; spine blocked with title and author's name in silver at head, 'Dent' blind at foot, reading across; all edges cut; top edge stained rust-red; end-papers white; issued in a scarlet and white dust-wrapper—front and spine white lettering on scarlet ground, back scarlet on white.

Collation: 254 pp. consisting: (1)–(2) half-title, verso list of books by the same author; (3)–(4) title, verso ' . . . First Published 1940'; (5)–(6) Contents, verso blank; 7–254 text; (255)–(256) printers' imprint, verso blank.

Publication. 1,500 copies were published on 4th Apr. 1940, at 7s. 6d. This impression did not go out of print until Feb. 1948, but the 2nd and 3rd impressions in Mar. and Dec. 1954 (of which the price was increased to 10s. 6d.) totalled 6,100 copies, and this in spite of the Guild Book edition of 50,250 copies in 1949 at 1s. Later impressions than the first are identifiable by verso of title.

Contents. The Peaches—A Visit to Grandpa's—Patricia, Edith and Arnold—the Fight—Extraordinary Little Cough—Just Like Little Dogs—Where Tawe Flows—Who Do You Wish Was With Us?—Old Garbo—One Warm Saturday.

Of these stories the following had earlier appeared in periodicals, mostly with slight variations (*see* Section C):

The Peaches—A Visit to Grandpa's—Old Garbo—Extraordinary

Little Cough—Just like Little Dogs—The Fight—Patricia, Edith and Arnold (the order in which they originally appeared).

This book has appeared in French, Italian, Danish, and Swedish translations (*see* Section E).

B. 7   PORTRAIT OF THE ARTIST AS A YOUNG DOG

American edition.
(Five red stars) PORTRAIT | (three red stars) OF THE ARTIST | (two red stars) AS A YOUNG DOG | BY DYLAN THOMAS | (space) | (five red stars; publisher's emblem) NORFOLK, CONN. | A NEW DIRECTIONS BOOK.

Demy 8vo (8¾″ × 5¾″), brick red cloth, spine blocked in gold with title reading downwards and publisher's imprint horizontal at foot; all edges cut; end-papers white; issued in a cream dust-wrapper printed in green, red, and black.

Collation: 186 pp. consisting: one blank leaf; (1)–(2) title, verso 'Copyright 1940 by New Directions . . .'; (3)–(4) Contents, verso blank; (5)–(6) half-title, verso blank; 7–186 text; (187)–(188) recto blank, verso colophon: ' (three stars) Printed for New Directions | by the Walpole Printing Office at Mount | Vernon, N.Y., in September 1940.   The | type is Weiss, the paper Champlain Text.'; one blank leaf.   (Cream laid paper throughout.)

Publication.   1,000 copies were published on 24th Sept. 1940, at $2.50.   The second impression, consisting of 2,000 copies at $3.00 each, was published in 1950 to celebrate Thomas's first visit to the United States, and differs from the earlier printing as follows: page size 8″ × 5″, yellow covers with fawn spine lettered in yellow (no imprint at foot), leaf preceding title here bears an extra half-title (verso blank), ornamental stars on title are black, verso of title bears the additional note 'Second Printing, 1950,' p.(188) is blank, printed on wove paper, dust-wrapper yellow printed in blank.

Contents.   As B. 6.

B. 8   FROM IN MEMORY OF ANN JONES
(Caseg Broadsheet No. 5)

CASEG BROADSHEET No. 5 | From | IN MEMORY | OF ANN JONES | (text)—alongside drawing by Brenda Chamberlain) | DYLAN THOMAS | Drawing by Brenda Chamberlain | With

acknowledgments to Mr Dylan Thomas and J. M. Dent & Sons for
permission to reprint this poem from *The Map of Love*. | (rule) | Pub-
lished by the Caseg Press, Llanllechid, Caernarvonshire and printed at
the Gomerian Press, Llandyssul, S. Wales.

One sheet, quarto ($10\frac{7}{8}'' \times 7\frac{3}{8}''$), printed on one side only.

Publication. The exact day of publication cannot be established
conclusively, but it was probably 2nd June 1942. 500 copies were
printed on 1st June 1942, and the British Museum copy was received
on 3rd June 1942.

As the title suggests, the poem is not here reprinted *in toto* and in
fact lacks the first nine lines. There is also one word difference from
The Map of Love version (*see* A. 64), though this may be a misprint.
The drawing by Brenda Chamberlain was executed specially for this
broadsheet and has not appeared since, either accompanying the poem
or elsewhere. (*See plate facing p. 32.*)

The Caseg Broadsheets were issued as the result of an idea by, and
collaboration of, Alun Lewis, John Petts, and Brenda Chamberlain.
All the broadsheets are now scarce, even if mainly on account of their
physical frailty.

B. 9   NEW POEMS

Dylan   Thomas | NEW   POEMS | (space) | Published   by | THE
POETS OF THE YEAR | NEW DIRECTIONS, NORFOLK, CONN.

Demy 8vo ($8\frac{5}{8}'' \times 6''$), mauve boards, author's name and title on front
cover; all edges cut; end-papers white. Issued in a mauve dust-
wrapper which was identical with the covers of the wrappered issue
(see *Publication* below). The board issue has an extra sheet of paper of
a different texture forming free end-papers at front and back.

Collation: 32 pp., unnumbered, made up of one gathering of 16
leaves, consisting: (1)–(2) half-title, verso blank; (3)–(4) title,
verso acknowledgments and ' . . . Copyright 1943 by New Directions . . . '; (5)–(29) text of the poems, (30) blank; (31)–(32)
colophon, verso note of the 1941 and 1942 volumes in the same series.

Publication. 2,500 copies were issued in Feb. 1943 (exact date
uncertain); of these, 1,000 were in paper boards and 1,500 in wrappers,
both styles being published simultaneously. Prices were (boards)
$1.00 and (wrappers) 50c.

Contents. There was a saviour—Into her lying down head—And
death shall have no dominion—Among those Killed in the Dawn
Raid—To Others than You—Love in the Asylum—The Marriage of a

Virgin—When I woke—The Hunchback in the Park—On a Wedding
Anniversary—Unluckily for a death—Ballad of the Long-Legged Bait—
Because the pleasure bird whistles—Once below a time—Request to
Leda—Deaths and Entrances—O make me a mask and a wall.

New Poems was designed at The Elm Tree Press of Mr William
Rudge, in Woodstock, Vermont, and was in fact first printed there.
Unfortunately, however, an error resulted in the page size of the book
being at variance with the other volumes in the 'Poets of the Month'
series and in consequence this first printing had to be destroyed.
Mr Rudge then had the edition reprinted in the correct format at his
family's press in New York City. As far as is known the entire first
printing was destroyed, but it may well be that one or two sets of the
unbound sheets survived somewhere.

B. 10   DEATHS AND ENTRANCES

DEATHS AND ENTRANCES | Poems by | DYLAN THOMAS |
(space) | LONDON: J. M. DENT & SONS LTD.

Demy 16mo ($5\frac{1}{2}'' \times 4\frac{1}{2}''$), deep orange cloth, spine blocked with title
and author's name in gold reading downwards, top edge cut, fore and
bottom edges trimmed but not evenly, end-papers white; issued in a
vermilion dust-wrapper lettered in black (i.e. front and spine vermilion,
back white).

Collation: 66 pp. consisting: (1)–(2) half-title, verso blank; (3)–(4)
title, verso '. . . First published 1946'; 5–(6) Contents, verso blank;
7–66 text of the poems; one blank leaf.

Publication. 3,000 copies were published on 7th Feb. 1946, at
3s. 6d. So far there have been four further impressions; these are
identifiable by a 'reprinted' note on verso of title, though the number
of the impression is not mentioned in all cases. The first three
impressions were printed on a rather inferior wove paper, due to
wartime paper restrictions, and bound in a deep orange cloth; the
4th and 5th impressions (Jan. 1954 and Apr. 1955) are on Antique
Laid paper—the same as that of the limited edition of *Collected Poems*—
with all edges cut, and bound in red cloth. The price was increased
to 4s. 6d. in Feb. 1947, 5s. in Jan. 1952, and 6s. in Jan. 1954.

Contents. The Conversation of Prayer—A Refusal to Mourn the
Death, by Fire, of a Child in London—Poem in October ('It was my
thirtieth year to heaven')—This Side of the Truth—To Others than
You—Love in the Asylum—Unluckily for a Death—The Hunchback
in the Park—Into her Lying Down Head—Paper and Sticks—Deaths

and Entrances—A Winter's Tale—On a Wedding Anniversary—There
was a Saviour—On the Marriage of a Virgin—In my Craft or Sullen
Art—Ceremony After a Fire Raid—When I Woke—Among those
Killed in the Dawn Raid was a Man Aged a Hundred—Lie Still, Sleep
Becalmed—Vision and Prayer—Ballad of the Long-legged Bait—Holy
Spring—Fern Hill.

All these poems had previously appeared in various periodicals (*see*
Section C).

B. 11   SELECTED WRITINGS

SELECTED WRITINGS OF | DYLAN THOMAS | INTRODUCTION
BY JOHN L. SWEENEY | (space) | A NEW DIRECTIONS BOOK

Demy 8vo (8⅜″ × 5¼″), pinkish mauve cloth, spine blocked at head with
author's name in gold within solid black oblong, reading downwards;
all edges cut, top edge stained mauve; end-papers white; issued in a
pale red dust-wrapper with titling matter in white and black.

Collation : 184 pp. consisting: (i)–(ii) half-title, verso blank; (iii)–
(iv) title, verso ' . . . Copyright 1946|by New Directions . . . ';
v–vi Contents, verso continued; (vii)–(viii) 'INTRODUCTION,'
verso blank; tipped-in frontis., recto blank, verso portrait by Augustus
John; ix–xxiii text of the Introduction, (xxiv) blank; (1)–(2)
'POEMS,' verso blank; 3–91 text of the poems, (92) blank; (93)–
(94) 'STORIES,' verso blank; 95–137 text of the stories, (138)
blank; (139)–(140) 'STORIES | FROM ''PORTRAIT OF THE |
ARTIST AS A YOUNG DOG,''' verso blank; 141–183 text of the
stories, 184 Bibliography.

Publication. 4,000 copies were published on 8th Nov. 1946, at
$3.50. Reprints are identifiable only by the dust-wrapper which has
the printing number stated on the front flap.

Contents. Introduction; Poems: I see the boys of summer—The
force that through the green fuse—When, like a running grave—When
once the twilight locks no longer—Especially when the October wind—
From love's first fever—A process in the weather of the heart—I
dreamed my genesis—I, in my intricate image—A grief ago—Then
was my neophyte—From the oracular archives—Let the tale's sailor
from a Christian voyage—I make this in a warring absence—It is the
sinners' dust-tongued bell—The spire cranes—After the funeral—
How shall my animal—A saint about to fall—If my head hurt a hair's
foot—This bread 1 break—Hold hard, these ancient minutes—Today,
this insect, and the world I breathe—The hand that signed the paper—
Do you not father me—Foster the light—Twenty-four years remind

the tears of my eyes—When all my five and country senses see—There was a saviour—And death shall have no dominion—Among those Killed in the Dawn Raid—Love in the Asylum—Ballad of the Long-Legged Bait—Once below a time—Deaths and Entrances—The Marriage of a Virgin—Ceremony after a Fire Raid—Holy Spring—Vision and Prayer—Poem in October—Fern Hill—The Conversation of Prayers—A Winter's Tale—This side of the Truth—A Refusal to Mourn—Lie still, sleep becalmed—In my craft or sullen art; Stories: The Orchards—A Prospect of the Sea—The Burning Baby—The Mouse and the Woman—The Peaches—One Warm Saturday.

All these poems and stories are selected from Thomas's earlier books.

B. 12 PORTRAIT OF THE ARTIST AS A YOUNG DOG

Guild Books edition.
GUILD BOOKS No. 250 | (rule) | PORTRAIT OF THE ARTIST | AS A YOUNG DOG | by | DYLAN THOMAS | (space) | GUILD (device) BOOKS | Published for | THE BRITISH PUBLISHERS GUILD | By J. M. Dent & Sons Ltd., Bedford Street, London.

Foolscap 8vo (7⅛″ × 4⅜″); pink and green paper wrappers lettered on front, back and spine in black, Guild Books imprint on front cover in white; all edges cut; no end-papers; earliest copies (and latest) were issued without dust-wrapper.

Collation: 128 pp. consisting: (1)–(2) half-title, verso 'By the same author . . . '; (3)–(4) title, verso ' . . . First Published in Guild Books 1948 . . . '; (5)–(6) Contents, verso blank; 7–128 text.

Publication. 50,250 copies were published in Mar. 1949 (not 1948 as verso of title suggests), at 1s. In Feb. 1951 copies started to appear in a four-colour dust-wrapper with the increased price of 1s. 6d. printed on the front cover and front flap of this; a yellow blank label was at this time pasted over the 'ONE SHILLING' on the front cover of the book itself. Only 10,000 of these coloured wrappers were printed, however, and when the wrappered stock was exhausted in Sept. 1952 the book reassumed its original unwrappered style and price.

Contents. Same as B. 6.

This volume of poems by Dylan Thomas was printed
in Griffo type by Hans Mardersteig on the hand-press
of the Officina Bodoni in Verona, for James Laughlin
and J. M. Dent & Sons, Ltd. The edition consists of
ten copies on Japanese vellum, numbered I to X, and
140 copies on Fabriano hand-made paper, numbered
11 to 150, of which numbers 11 to 60 are for sale in
Great Britain, all signed by the author.
December Mcmxxxxix

Dylan Thomas

This copy is **Number**
60

DYLAN THOMAS

TWENTY-SIX POEMS

J. M. DENT & SONS LTD.
LONDON

B. 13   TWENTY-SIX POEMS

(a) *English issue.*
DYLAN   THOMAS | TWENTY-SIX | POEMS | (space) | J.   M.
DENT & SONS LTD. | LONDON.

4to (11¾″ × 8″), decorative boards (black and green repetitive design
on white ground), canvas back with white paper label at head lettered
in black 'DYLAN THOMAS (dot) POEMS' reading downwards;
headbands top and bottom; top edge trimmed, fore and bottom edges
untrimmed; end-papers white; issued in a grey board slip-case with no
labels or titling.

Collation: two blank leaves; (1)–(2) half-title, verso blank; (3)–(4)
title, verso copyright details and 'PRINTED IN ITALY'; 5–6 Contents,
verso continued; (7)–(8) 'TWENTY-SIX POEMS,' verso blank;
9–76 text of the poems; (77)–(78) recto blank, verso colophon: 'This
volume of poems by Dylan Thomas was printed | in Griffo type by
Hans Mardersteig on the hand-press | of the Officina Bodoni in
Verona for James Laughlin | and J. M. Dent & Sons, Ltd.   The
edition consists of | ten copies on Japanese vellum, numbered I to
X, and | 140 copies on Fabriano hand-made paper, numbered | 11 to
150, of which numbers 11 to 60 are for sale in | Great Britain, all
signed by the author. | December MCMXXXXIX | (printer's device
in red) | (author's signature) | This copy is Number | (number
printed)'; one blank leaf.

Publication.   The entire edition of this book was received at the
House of Dent in Jan. 1950.   The copies for New Directions were
re-dispatched from London in Mar. 1950, and the English issue was
published on 31st Aug. 1950, at £5 5s. (the whole of this issue being
sold on publication day).   The actual distribution of the entire edition,
English and American copies, was as follows:

1–2 (Jap. vellum)	:	author's free copies.
3–10 ,, ,,	:	to New Directions.
11–60 (H/made paper)	:	to Dent.
61–147 ,, ,,	:	to New Directions.
148–149 ,, ,,	:	author's free copies.
150 ,, ,,	:	Dent file copy.

Contents.   I see the boys of summer—Especially when the October
wind—From love's first fever—A process in the weather of the heart—
I, in my intricate image—Then was my neophyte—I make this in a
warring absence—It is the sinners' dust-tongued bell—After the
funeral—How shall my animal—If my head hurt a hair's foot—This
bread I break—Hold hard, these ancient minutes—Today, this insect—

The hand that signed the paper—Twenty-four years remind the tears
of my eyes—When all my five and country senses see—There was a
saviour—Ballad of the Long-Legged Bait—Deaths and Entrances—Fern
Hill—A Winter's Tale—A Refusal to Mourn—Lie still, sleep becalmed
—In my craft or sullen art—In Country Sleep.

(See plates between pp. 52 and 53.)

(*b*) *American issue.*

The American copies are identical with the English with one
exception, viz. no publisher's imprint appears on the title page.   The
exact publication date in U.S.A. is not recorded, but the American
issue undoubtedly preceded the English issue by about three months,
appearing towards the end of the second week in May 1950.   Evidence
further suggests that the vellum copies preceded the hand-made paper
issue by about two days.

Prices were: vellum, $25.00; hand-made paper, $15.00.

B. 14   IN COUNTRY SLEEP

Limited edition.

IN COUNTRY SLEEP | and other poems by DYLAN THOMAS |
(photograph   portrait   by   Marion   Morehouse) | A   NEW
DIRECTIONS BOOK.

Crown 8vo (8½″ × 6″), buff-grey cloth blocked in gold with author's
name (at head) and title (at foot) on front cover and the same on spine
reading downwards; all edges cut, top edge stained rust-brown; end-
papers white; issued in a dark brown card slip-case bearing a white
label on front with a border and titling in red, opening to the left with
cutaway finger pieces.

Collation: 34 + (2) pp. consisting: (i)–(ii) 'This is number'
(number in ink) 'of one hundred copies | printed on Stoneridge paper
and | signed by the author | (signature) | (space),' verso blank;
(1)–(2) title, verso 'Copyright 1952 by Dylan Thomas . . .'; (3)–
(4) acknowledgments to periodicals, and to photographer, verso
blank; (5)–(6) Contents, verso blank; (7)–(8) half-title, verso blank;
9–34 text of the poems; (35)–(36) recto blank, verso colophon:
' . . . one hundred copies on Stoneridge paper . . . signed . . . and
five thousand copies on Kilmory paper . . . '; one blank leaf.

Publication. 100 copies were published on 28th Feb. 1952, at
$7.50.

Contents. Over Sir John's Hill—Poem on His Birthday—Do Not
Go Gentle into That Good Night—Lament—In the White Giant's
Thigh—In Country Sleep.

B. 15   IN COUNTRY SLEEP

Ordinary edition.
IN COUNTRY SLEEP | and other poems by DYLAN THOMAS |
(photograph portrait by Marion Morehouse) | A NEW
DIRECTIONS BOOK.

Crown 8vo (8½" × 6"), greenish slate-coloured boards, blocked in
brown with author's name (at head) and title (at foot) on front cover
and likewise on spine reading downwards; all edges cut, white; end-
papers white; issued in a cream dust-wrapper lettered in rust-brown.
   Collation : identical with the limited edition except for p. (i) which
is blank.
   Publication.   5,000 copies were published on the same day as the
limited edition—28th Feb. 1952—at $2.00.
   Contents.   As limited edition.
   The paper of this issue varies from B. 14, as described in the colophon.

B. 16   COLLECTED POEMS

First (English) edition, ordinary issue.
DYLAN   THOMAS | Collected   Poems | 1934–1952 | (space) |
LONDON | J. M. DENT & SONS LTD.

Demy 8vo (8⅜" × 5⅜"), issued in dark blue cloth, spine blocked with
author's name and title at head and 'Dent' at foot in gold; all edges
cut; top edge stained rust-red; end-papers white; issued in a sandy-
grey dust-wrapper lettered in red with white panels on spine and white
ornamental line on front cover, back cover white lettered in black.
   Collation : 178 pp. consisting: pp. (i)–(ii) half-title, verso list of
books by the same author; tipped-in frontis. (portrait by Augustus John)
recto blank; (iii)–(iv) title, verso ' . . . First published 1952'; (v)–
(vi) dedication 'TO | CAITLIN,' verso author's note; vii–x 'Author's
Prologue' (in verse); xi–xiv Contents; 1–178 text of the poems.
   Publication.   4,760 copies were published on 10th Nov. 1952, at
12s. 6d.   With the 8th impression (Jan. 1955) the book reached
30,800 copies.   A few weeks prior to publication 68 proof copies
were printed; these have the leaves which ultimately bore the 'Author's
Prologue' blank except for the word 'Preface' on p. (v), also the
dedication and 'Note' on its verso are lacking (pp. (v)–(vi) in the
trade edition) but the total number of pages is the same since the poem
'Paper and Sticks' appears on p. 116, necessitating an extra leaf at

the end of the volume to accommodate the whole of the last poem. The excision of 'Paper and Sticks' before publication resulted in a slight rearrangement of a few poems, but, although 'Do not go gentle into that good night' was moved back to p. 116 the order remained generally speaking chronological otherwise. The proof copies were issued in pale green paper wrappers printed in black.

After and including the 8th impression a slightly enlarged form of contents table was used, incorporating titles *and* first lines.[1]

Contents. The whole of *18 Poems*, the whole of *Twenty-Five Poems*, the whole of *Deaths and Entrances* except 'Paper and Sticks,' all the poems from *The Map of Love*, and also the following poems which had not previously appeared in a book by Thomas published in Great Britain in an unlimited edition: 'Do not go gentle into that good night'—'In Country Sleep'—'Over Sir John's Hill'—'Poem on His Birthday'—'Lament'—'In the White Giant's Thigh'—'Prologue.' A large number of the poems differ from their earlier versions; these variations are set out in Section A.

(See plate facing p. 72.)

B. 17   COLLECTED POEMS

First (English) edition, limited issue.
This differed from the ordinary issue only in the binding, paper, and note on verso of title.

Issued in full dark blue crushed morocco (blocked on spine as ordinary issue), top edge gilt instead of rust-red, headbands top and bottom. Verso of title reads: ' . . . First published 1952 | This edition, printed | on mould-made paper, | is limited to 65 copies, | of which 60 are for sale. | This copy is No. . . . (number in ink) | (author's signature).' Issued in a plain cellophane dust-wrapper.

Published on the same day as the ordinary issue, at £5 5s.

(See plate facing p. 24.)

B. 18   COLLECTED POEMS

American edition.
THE | COLLECTED | POEMS | OF | DYLAN | THOMAS | A NEW DIRECTIONS BOOK.

Demy 8vo (8½″ × 5½″), blue cloth, spine lettered with title in black and author's name in silver reading downwards; all edges cut; endpapers white; issued in a white dust-wrapper printed in black.

---

[1] This form of the 'Contents,' however, appeared five weeks earlier in the copies printed for the Readers Union.   *See* B. 25, *Readers Union Edition.*

Collation: 199 pp. consisting: one blank leaf; (i)–(ii) half-title, verso blank; (iii)–(iv) list of books by Thomas, verso blank; tipped-in frontis. (photo by Marion Morehouse), recto blank; (v)–(vi) title, verso ' . . . Copyright 1952, 1953 by Dylan Thomas . . . '; vii–x Contents; (xi)–(xii) dedication, verso blank; (xiii)–(xiv) Note by the author, verso blank; xv–xviii Author's Prologue (verse); (xix)–(xx) 'The Collected Poems of Dylan Thomas,' verso blank; 1–199 text of the poems, (200) blank; one blank leaf.

Publication.   6,000 copies were published on 31st Mar. 1953, at $3.75.   Reprints can be identified by the correct printing of the word 'daughters' on p. 199, this being a misprint in the first impression. Otherwise the dust-wrapper mentions the impression number on the front flap.   Two other misprints were corrected in the third and sixth printings.

Contents.   As English edition.

B. 19   THE DOCTOR AND THE DEVILS

First (English) edition.
THE   DOCTOR | AND   THE   DEVILS | by | DYLAN   THOMAS | from   the   story   by | DONALD   TAYLOR | (space) | LONDON | J. M. DENT & SONS LTD.

Crown 8vo ($7\frac{1}{4}''$ × $4\frac{3}{4}''$), red cloth lettered across spine with author's name, title, and 'Dent' in gold; all edges cut; end-papers white; issued in a black, greyish-buff and white pictorial dust-wrapper with author's name in red long-hand.

Collation: 138 pp. consisting: (i)–(ii) half-title and, at foot, 9-line note on the basis of the story, verso 'By the same author . . . ' (iii)–(iv) title, verso ' . . . First published 1953 | (space) | (3-line note)'; 1–134 text of the film scenario; 135–138 'The Story of the Film' by Donald Taylor; one blank leaf.

Publication.   4,000 copies were published on 14th May 1953, at 10s. 6d.   Of the second impression of 2,500 copies 1,500 were sold with a cancel title to New Directions and form the 2nd, or 1st American edition.   Verso of title identifies each impression.

35 proof copies of this book were printed in mid 1947 in which the character 'Rock' of the final version appears as 'Salter.'   In point of fact this character was originally 'Knox' but was substituted at James Bridie's suggestion.   Production was halted after 1947 until Apr. 1953, when 97 further proofs were printed—this time with the final 'Rock.'   The early proof copies are now extremely rare, and it is impossible to guess how many of the original 35 are still extant; they

bear the date '1947' on verso of title apart from the alteration of the character name, and are also slimmer than the 1953 proofs and bound in stiff cork-coloured wrappers as against the pale green flimsier paper of the later printing.

B. 20   THE DOCTOR AND THE DEVILS

(a) *American edition.   First issue.*

This issue was identical with the English edition with three small exceptions:

1. Title has the imprint of New Directions at foot in place of that of Dent.
2. This issue being printed off from the second English impression the 'Reprinted . . . ' note on verso of title was excised and the biblio adapted.
3. Foot of spine has New Directions imprint in place of that of Dent. Spine of dust-wrapper was similarly amended, also front flap to show dollar price.

Publication.   1,500 copies were published on 8th Oct. 1953, at $2.50.   All were imported, made up.

(b) *American edition.   Second issue.*

This issue was printed by photo-litho from the first American issue, but to a slightly larger scale: page measurements are 8″ × 5¼″.   Collation is the same, but binding is of grey imitation cloth (glossy grey paper, grained, on boards), with title and author's name on spine in white reading across—no imprint at foot.   All edges are cut and end-papers are white as before, but a new dust-wrapper was designed—plain white, lettered in black, titling matter on front enclosed within an irregular grey figure, and the words 'Second Printing' at head of front flap.

Publication.   Of this issue 2,000 copies were published at $3.00, earliest copies leaving the publisher's warehouse towards the end of Dec. 1953.

B. 21   UNDER MILK WOOD

First (English) edition.

DYLAN   THOMAS | (star) | Under   Milk   Wood | A   Play   for Voices | (space) | Preface   and   musical   settings   by | DANIEL JONES | (space) | LONDON | J. M. DENT & SONS LTD.

Crown 8vo ($7\frac{1}{4}'' \times 4\frac{3}{4}''$), light brown cloth; spine blocked with title and author's name at head, 'Dent' at foot, reading across, in gold; all edges cut; end-papers white (but there is no back free end-paper); issued in an apple-green dust-wrapper lettered in black on front and spine (enclosed within white border on front) with photo of the author on back.

Collation: 101 pp. consisting: (i)–(ii) half-title, verso list of other books by Thomas; (iii)–(iv) title, verso ' . . . First published 1954,' etc. (note on copyright and performing rights); v–viii Preface; ix–x Contents, verso blank; 1–86 text of the play; 87–88 Notes on Pronunciation; 89–90 full cast of the first broadcast; 91–92 'SONGS | (Music by Daniel Jones)', verso blank; 93–101 music and words of the songs, (102) blank.

Publication. 6,400 copies were published on 5th Mar. 1954, at 8s. 6d. Subsequent impressions are identifiable by verso of title. The 7th impression, in May 1955, brought the number of copies printed of this English edition up to 53,700.

Presages of *Under Milk Wood* can be found in several of Thomas's earlier works of which perhaps the most concrete is the story *Quite Early One Morning*, published in Autumn 1946 (*see* C. 159). Various articles in the Dylan Thomas Memorial Number of *Adam* (C. 183) establish other aspects of the history of this play, but the first revelation of the author's plans for the whole work appeared in *Botteghe Oscure*, No. 9, 1952 (C. 175) in which nearly half of the play, with certain variations towards the end, was published under the title 'LLAREGGUB: A Piece for Radio Perhaps,' followed by a note by Thomas outlining his hopes and intentions regarding the final version. The play was performed several times prior to publication, and broadcast, but the first published indication of the book to come was given by *Mademoiselle* and the *Observer* in Feb. 1954 (C. 185/6/7).

(*See plate facing p. 17.*)

B. 22   UNDER MILK WOOD

American edition.
Dylan Thomas | UNDER MILK WOOD | A PLAY FOR VOICES | (space) | A NEW DIRECTIONS BOOK.

Crown 8vo ($8'' \times 5''$), mulberry-brown cloth, spine lettered in white with title and author's name reading downwards; all edges cut; end-papers white; issued in a glossy black dust-wrapper with green and white abstract design and white lettering on front and spine, note on Thomas and photo on back (black on white).

Collation: 107 pp. consisting: one blank leaf; (i)–(ii) half-title, verso list of other books by Thomas; tipped-in frontis. (photo by Rollie McKenna), recto blank; (iii)–(iv) title, verso 'Copyright 1954 by New Directions . . . '; (v)–(vi) Contents, verso blank; vii–xi Preface by Daniel Jones, (xii) blank; xiii–xiv Note on a trial performance on 14th May 1953 in New York City, with cast of characters, verso cast continued; (xv)–(xvi) 'UNDER MILK WOOD,' verso blank; 1–95 text of the play; (96) blank; 97–98 Notes on Pronunciation; (99) blank; 100–107 Music for the Songs, (108) blank; one blank leaf.

Publication. 6,000 copies were published on 28th Apr. 1954, at $3.00.

B. 23   QUITE EARLY ONE MORNING

English edition.
QUITE   EARLY | ONE   MORNING | broadcasts   by | DYLAN THOMAS | preface   by | ANEIRIN   TALFAN   DAVIES | Welsh Region,   B.B.C. | (space) | LONDON | J.   M.   DENT & SONS LTD.

Crown 8vo ($7\frac{1}{4}$" × $4\frac{3}{4}$"), blue cloth; spine blocked with author's name, title, and 'DENT' in gold reading across; all edges cut; endpapers white; issued in a blue dust-wrapper lettered white on front and black on spine, photo of Thomas at microphone on front (a retouched facsimile of the frontis.).

Collation: 181 pp. consisting: (i)–(ii) half-title, verso list of books by the same author; tipped-in frontis (photo of Thomas in a B.B.C. studio); (iii)–(iv) title, verso ' . . . First published 1954'; v–vi Contents; vii–x Preface and Acknowledgments; 1–170 text of the broadcasts; 171–181 Notes, (182) blank.

Publication. 10,000 copies were published on 4th Nov. 1954, at 10s. 6d.

On pp. 3 and 11 of the first impression there is a full stop after 'sailors' at the end of verse 5 of 'The Hunchback in the Park'; this was modified to a comma in subsequent impressions. Several other errors were corrected after the second impression, but the number of each impression is primarily indicated by the verso of title.

Contents. Reminiscences of Childhood (First Version)—Reminiscences of Childhood (Second Version)—Quite Early One Morning—Memories of Christmas—Holiday Memory—How to Begin a Story—The Crumbs of One Man's Year—The Festival Exhibition, 1951—The International Eisteddfod—A Visit to America—Laugharne—Return Journey—Wilfred Owen—Walter de la Mare as a Prose Writer—Sir

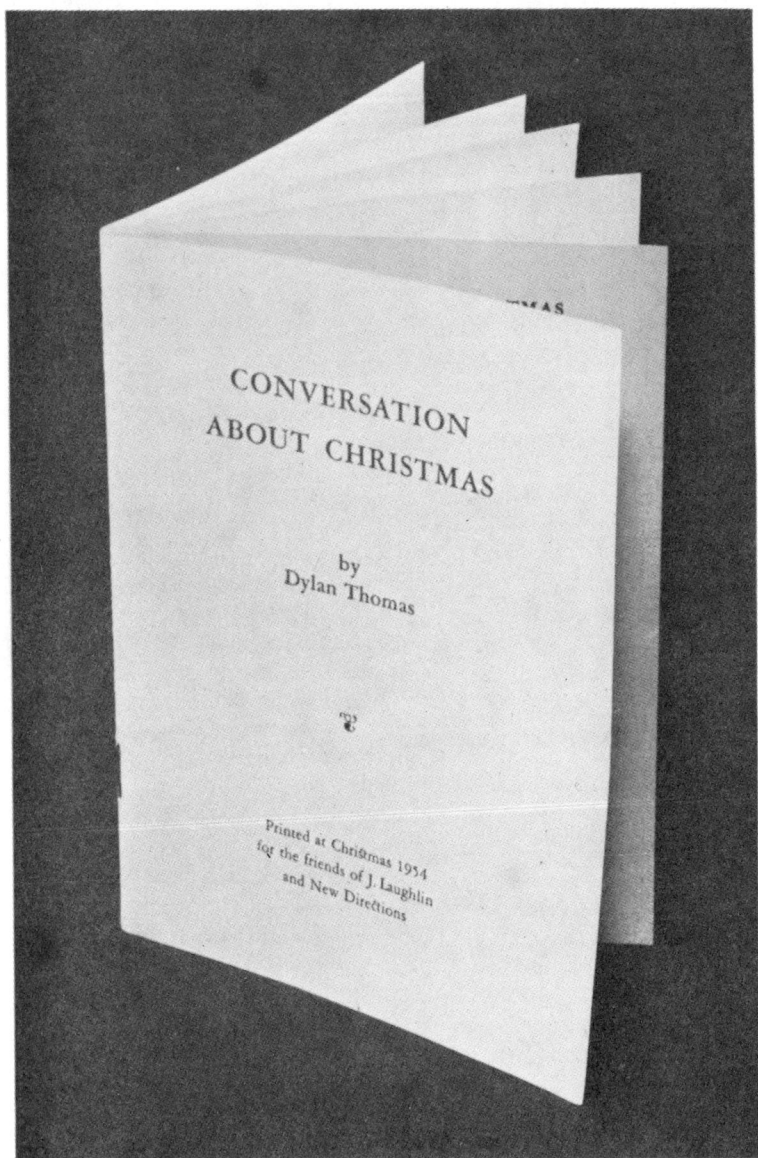

Philip Sidney—A Dearth of Comic Writers—The English Festival of
Spoken Poetry—On Reading One's Own Poems—Welsh Poets—
Wales and the Artist—Three Poems—On Poetry—*Notes*.

The version of the story *Quite Early One Morning* is, as explained in
the *Notes*, that of the repeat broadcast; this varies somewhat at the end
from the earlier version and the differences, including the deleted
verse of the poem, are described in the *Notes* in detail.   The *Notes*
are of great interest throughout and give, amongst other things, the
dates of the broadcasts, including repeats.

It should be noted that the American edition of this title cannot be
regarded properly as the 'second edition' since its contents differ
considerably from this one (*see* B. 24).

B. 24   QUITE EARLY ONE MORNING

American edition.
Dylan   Thomas | QUITE | EARLY | ONE | MORNING | A   New
Directions Book.

Crown 8vo (8″ × 5⅜″), grey cloth spine blocked in white with author's
name and title reading downwards; all edges cut; end-papers white;
issued in a black and white pictorial dust-wrapper (photo of Thomas
at Laugharne) with titling in yellow overprinted.

Collation: 240 pp. consisting: one blank leaf; (i)–(ii) half-title,
verso list of books by Thomas; (iii)–(iv) title, verso 'Copyright 1954
by New Directions . . . '; v–(vi) Contents, verso blank; vii–viii
Publisher's Note, verso continued; (1)–(2) 'PART I,' verso blank;
3–93 text, (94) blank; (95)–(96) 'PART II,' verso blank; 97–240
text; three blank leaves.

Publication. 3,200 copies were published on 15th Dec. 1954.
Subsequent impressions are identifiable only by a note on the front
flap of the dust-wrapper.   Of the third impression of 5,000 copies in
Jan. 1955, 2,500 were for the 'Atlantic Monthly Book Club.'

Contents.   Reminiscences of Childhood—Quite Early One Morning
—A Child's Christmas in Wales—Holiday Memory—A Story—The
Crumbs of One Man's Year—Laugharne—Return Journey—Our
Country—Welsh Poets—Wilfred Owen—Sir Philip Sidney—Artists of
Wales—Walter de la Mare as a Prose Writer—A Dearth of Comic
Writers—The English Festival of Spoken Poetry—On Reading One's
Own Poems—Three Poems—Replies to an Enquiry—On Poetry—
How to be a Poet—How to Begin a Story—The Festival Exhibition,
1951—The International Eisteddfod—A Visit to America.

By comparing the above with the English edition it will be seen that
F

a number of extra pieces are included here, whilst there are at the same time two exclusions ('Reminiscences of Childhood, first version' and 'Notes'). Of the pieces common to both editions, versions are identical except for the following:

'Quite Early One Morning': A few punctuation differences and more paragraphing.

'A Child's Christmas in Wales': This is the *Harper's Bazaar* version (C. 170), being 'Memories of Christmas' with 'Conversation About Christmas' inserted in the middle and adapted somewhat to suit the arrangement.

'Holiday Memory': Less paragraphing.

'The Crumbs of One Man's Year': Slightly more paragraphing.

'The International Eisteddfod': One paragraph is here broken into two.

'How to Begin a Story': Lacks 'Announcer's' words at end.

'Sir Philip Sidney': The old English spelling in quotations is here preserved in places.

'The English Festival of Spoken Poetry': One paragraph is here broken into two.

'Welsh Poets': Several extra paragraphs added and four more poems by Alun Lewis quoted (though one quotation has only one verse in place of three).

'Artists of Wales': English title was 'Wales and the Artist.' Text is identical.

'Three Poems': Two only; 'In Country Sleep' omitted.

B. 25   COLLECTED POEMS

Readers Union edition.

DYLAN THOMAS | (ornament) | COLLECTED | POEMS | (ornament) | 1934–1952 (all the above enclosed in ornamental border) | READERS UNION | J. M. DENT & SONS | LONDON 1954.

Post 8vo (8" × 4⅞"), light brown 3-Point Canvas, spine blocked as the Dent edition but with Readers Union device at foot in place of 'Dent'; all edges cut, top edge stained rust-red; end-papers white; issued in a white-decorated brown dust-wrapper with titling matter brown on white panels.

Collation: 178 pp. consisting: (i)–(ii) half-title, verso blank; tipped-in frontis., recto blank (as Dent edition); (iii)–(iv) title, verso '. . . produced in 1954 for sale to its members only by Readers Union Ltd. . . .'; (v)–(vi) dedication, verso author's note; vii–x 'Author's Prologue'; xi–xiv Contents; 1–178 text of the poems.

Publication. 3,500 copies were published on 4th Dec. 1954, as the

'Readers Union Extra Additional' for December. These were specially printed off by The Aldine Press, Letchworth, between the 7th and 8th impressions of the Dent edition, and differ from the latter only in binding, title, and size.   The Contents table is, however, the slightly expanded form of the Dent 8th impression of Jan. 1955, and the Readers Union edition thus constitutes the first issue of the book with this variation.

The edition was quickly sold out and to meet further demands a further 500 copies were made up from the Dent 9th impression (not published until May 1955) in Feb. 1955, and yet another 500 in July 1955.   These two issues were in a larger format than the first— the same size, in fact, as the Dent edition—and were bound in a finer 'Sundour' cloth of a slightly different shade of brown.   The price was 5s. 6d. for Readers Union members only, throughout the entire edition, and there is of course no printed mention of reprinting in the later issues.

This edition was announced as forthcoming in *Readers News* (The Magazine of Readers Union), Vol. 17, No. 5, Oct. 1954 (8 pp.) which also contains a specially written article on Thomas by Aneirin Talfan Davies entitled 'He Sang of Glory.'

(*See plate facing p. 65.*)

B. 26   CONVERSATION ABOUT CHRISTMAS

CONVERSATION | ABOUT   CHRISTMAS | by | Dylan   Thomas | (device) | Printed at Christmas 1954 | for the friends of J. Laughlin | and New Directions.

6″ × 4½″, 6 leaves stapled (including the 'cover' which is of very slightly thicker paper), all edges cut.

Collation: 8 pp. consisting: (i)–(ii) title, verso 'Copyright 1954 by New Directions | Printed by special arrangement | with the Trustees of the | Estate of Dylan Thomas'; pp. 1–8 text; pp. (9)–(10) 'Printed by Igal Roodenko and James Lanier, New York,' verso blank.

2,000 copies were printed in Dec. 1954 and distributed during the Christmas season to 'the friends of J. Laughlin and New Directions.' None was offered for sale.

The text is identical with that of the original, in *Picture Post*, 27th Dec. 1947 (*see* C. 164), and also with that of *A Prospect of the Sea*, pp. 97–103 (B. 28); this, however, constitutes the first separate edition.

(*See plate facing p. 61.*)

B. 27   ADVENTURES IN THE SKIN TRADE AND OTHER STORIES

Dylan   Thomas | ADVENTURES | IN   THE | SKIN   TRADE | and
other | stories | A   New   Directions   Book.

Crown 8vo (8″ × 5⅜″), grey cloth, spine blocked with author's name
and title *Adventures in the Skin Trade* in white reading downwards; all
edges cut; end-papers white; issued in a glossy dust-wrapper, the
front and spine having a photographic background of Thomas in his
room at Laugharne, titling overprinted in red, back white bearing
note on Thomas and portrait by Augustus John (monochrome).

Collation: 275 pp. consisting: (i)–(ii) half-title, verso list of books
by the same author; (iii)–(iv) title, verso 'Copyright 1955 by New
Directions . . . '; v–(vi) Contents, verso blank; vii–viii Publisher's
Note, verso (continued); (1)–(2) half-title repeated, verso blank;
3–275 text of the stories, (276) blank; two blank leaves.

Publication. 5,000 copies were published on 18th May 1955, at $3.50.

Contents. Adventures in the Skin Trade—After the Fair—The
Enemies—The Tree—The Visitor—The Lemon—The Burning Baby—
The Orchards—The Mouse and the Woman—The Horse's Ha—A
Prospect of the Sea—The Holy Six—Prologue to an Adventure—The
Map of Love—In the Direction of the Beginning—An Adventure from
a Work in Progress—The School for Witches—The Dress—The Vest
—The True Story—The Followers.

Of these stories the following appear here for the first time in book
form: Adventures in the Skin Trade (complete, i.e. all that Thomas
wrote)—After the Fair—The Lemon—The Horse's Ha—An Adventure
from a Work in Progress—The Vest—The True Story—The Followers.

'In the Direction of the Beginning' appears here for the first time
in a book by Thomas (earlier in *New Directions 1938*).

The remaining twelve stories are reprinted from either *The Map of
Love* or *The World I Breathe*.

B. 28   A PROSPECT OF THE SEA

A   PROSPECT | OF   THE   SEA | and   other   stories | and   prose
writings | by | DYLAN   THOMAS | Edited   by | DANIEL   JONES |
(space) | LONDON | J. M. DENT & SONS LTD.

Crown 8vo (7⅛″ × 4¾″), blue cloth; spine blocked in gold with
author's name, title, and 'DENT,' reading across; all edges cut; end-
papers white; issued in a pale blue dust-wrapper with a background

DYLAN THOMAS

COLLECTED
POEMS

1934–1952

READERS UNION

J. M. DENT & SONS

LONDON 1954

COLLECTED POEMS—title-page of Readers Union first edition (B. 25) of horizontal white wavy lines, lettered in black, with photo (as frontis.) on back.

Collation: 136 pp. consisting: (i)–(ii) half-title, verso list of other books by Thomas; tipped-in frontis. (photo of the author and his wife and daughter in a boat), recto blank; (iii)–(iv) title, verso ' . . . First published July 1955'; v–(vi) Publisher's Note, verso blank; vii–(viii) Contents, verso blank; (1)–(2) 'PART I,' verso blank; 3–94 text; (95)–(96) 'PART II,' verso blank; 97–136 text.

Publication. 8,000 copies were published on 28th July 1955, at 10s. 6d.   Reprints are noted on verso of title.

Contents.   A Prospect of the Sea—The Lemon—After the Fair—The Visitor—The Enemies—The Tree—The Map of Love—The Mouse and the Woman—The Dress —The Orchards—In the Direction of the Beginning—Conversation about Christmas—How to be a Poet—The Followers—A Story.

All of these prose pieces had appeared in book form previously elsewhere except 'How to be a Poet,' which, however, appeared in *Quite Early One Morning,* American edition, but in a slightly shortened form *(see* C. 167).   The story 'The Lemon' differs from the version in *Adventures in the Skin Trade and Other Stories* in that 'Doctor Manza' becomes simply 'the doctor.'

B. 29 ADVENTURES IN THE SKIN TRADE

Dylan   Thomas | Adventures | in   the | Skin | Trade | (publisher's device) | PUTNAM | 42 GREAT   RUSSELL   STREET | LONDON.

Crown 8vo ($7\frac{1}{4}'' \times 4\frac{7}{8}''$), black linson; spine blocked in gold with title and author's name in enclosure reading downwards, 'PUTNAM' at foot reading across; all edges cut; end-papers white; issued in a mauve, pink, black and white dust-wrapper (black and white lettering on abstract background design).

Collation: 115 pp. consisting: (1)–(2) half-title, verso blank; (3)–(4) title, verso 'First published in Great Britain 1955 . . . '; (5)–(6) 'Foreword | by | Vernon | Watkins,' verso blank; 7–14 Foreword; (15)–(16) 'Adventures | in the | Skin | Trade,' verso blank; 17–115 text, (116) blank.

Publication. 6,900 copies were published on 12th Sept. 1955, at 9s. 6d.   Verso of title notes reprints.

This constitutes the first separate edition of this unfinished novel. The history of the piece, and an outline of Thomas's plans for the whole (including his reasons for so titling the book) are to be found in Vernon Watkins's foreword.

B. 30   A CHILD'S CHRISTMAS IN WALES

A Child's | Christmas | in Wales | DYLAN THOMAS (the foregoing in red, free-hand) | (space) | NEW DIRECTIONS | NORFOLK · CONNECTICUT (black letter-press).

Crown 8vo (7¼" × 5"), pale grey boards with title in red and author's name in black on front cover, author's name and title in red on spine reading downwards; all edges cut; end-papers white; issued in a dust-wrapper of the same paper as covers the boards, and of identical design except for spine-lettering which is black.

Collation: 32 pp. consisting: one blank leaf; (1)–(2) title, verso 'Copyright 1954 by New Directions . . .'; (3)–(4) half-title, verso blank; 5–(32) text; (33)–(34) 'Lettering by Samuel H. Marsh,' verso blank.

Publication. 10,000 copies were published on 15th Dec. 1955, at $1.50. The book was printed for New Directions by Peter Beilenson at Mount Vernon, N.Y.

Contents. 'A Child's Christmas in Wales,' reprinted from the American edition of *Quite Early One Morning.* A special (first separate) edition produced for Christmas 1955.

B. 31   PORTRAIT OF THE ARTIST AS A YOUNG DOG

American cheap edition.
PORTRAIT OF THE ARTIST | AS A YOUNG DOG | by Dylan Thomas | (space) | A New Directions PAPERBOOK.

Foolscap 8vo (7⅛" × 4⅛"); black and white card wrappers lettered in black and white; all edges cut; no end-papers; no dust-wrapper.

Collation: 160 pp. consisting: (1)–(2) half-title, verso blank; (3)–(4) note on the author (27 lines), verso list of books by Thomas; (5)–(6) title, verso ' . . . First published as New Directions Paperbook No. 51, 1955. . . .'; (7)–(8) Contents, verso blank; 9–160 text.

Publication. As the copyright page suggests, publication was scheduled for 1955, but in fact the book was delayed and not finally issued until 25th Jan. 1956, when the first impression—of 15,900 copies—was published at 95c. per copy, as 'New Directions Paper-book' No. 51.

Contents. As B. 6.

SECTION C

Contributions by Dylan Thomas
to Periodicals

NOTE

THIS section includes only original contributions. Different versions of one poem or prose piece may be listed but no two items described are exactly alike as regards text.

Translations of work by Thomas are not mentioned beyond 1944. It is hoped that the few that are noted, up to 1944, will be of interest, but after that date they become too numerous to justify inclusion here and many are in any case none too readily accessible.

Items containing poems are cross-referenced to *Section A*, where more exact details of version can be found. Prose items are described rather more fully, followed by a note of first appearance in book form—if any.

It is fairly certain that Thomas contributed at least two reviews for the *Literary Review* in 1937, but these appear to have been signed or initialled pseudonymously, as were those by other contributors. The reviews may have been the result of collaboration with Ruthven Todd, with whom Thomas was closely associated at this time.

A number of stories will be found described as appearing for the first time in book form in *Adventures in the Skin Trade*; this is a slight contraction for the sake of space economy and refers in fact to *Adventures in the Skin Trade and Other Stories*, New Directions, 1955.

C. 1 *Swansea Grammar School Magazine*, Vol. 22, No. 3, Dec. 1925. p. 74: 'Song of a Mischievous Dog' (poem, 1 verse of 16 lines).

This poem was reprinted in *Adam*, Year 21, No. 238, 1953, p. 1.

C. 2 *Swansea Grammar School Magazine*, Vol. 23, No. 3, Dec. 1926. p. 76: 'His Repertoire' (poem, 1 verse of 28 lines).

This poem was reprinted in *Adam*, Year 21, No. 238, 1953, p. 1.

C. 2a *Western Mail*, 14th Jan. 1927.
p. 6: 'His Requiem' (poem, 2 verses of 2 and 16 lines).
Signed 'D. M. Thomas.'

C. 3 *Swansea Grammar School Magazine*, Vol. 24, No. 1, Mar. 1927.
pp. 16–17: 'The Watchers' (poem).

C. 4 *Swansea Grammar School Magazine*, Vol. 24, No. 2, July 1927.
p. 44: 'Best of All' (poem, 1 verse of 12 lines).
This poem was reprinted in *Adam*, Year 21, No. 238, 1953,
p. 2 and also p. 66. The versions on both these pages vary
slightly as regards punctuation from the original, that on p. 2
being the nearest to it.

C. 5 *Swansea Grammar School Magazine*, Vol. 25, No. 1, Mar. 1928.
p. 19: 'Forest Picture' (poem, 1 verse of 12 lines).
p. 14: 'School Memories by a Very Old "Boy"' (poem).
'Forest Picture' was reprinted in *Adam*, Year 21, No. 238,
1953, p. 2.

C. 6 *Swansea Grammar School Magazine*, Vol. 25, No. 2, July 1928.
p. 42: 'Life-belt' (poem).
p. 43: 'Missing' (poem).

C. 7 *Swansea Grammar School Magazine*, Vol. 25, No. 3, Dec. 1928.
p. 77: 'In dreams' (poem).

C. 8 *Swansea Grammar School Magazine*, Vol. 26, No. 1, Mar. 1929.
pp. 15–16: 'Idyll of unforgetfulness' (poem).

C. 9 *Swansea Grammar School Magazine*, Vol. 26, No. 2, July 1929.
p. 42: 'A Ballad of Salad' (poem).

C. 10 *Swansea Grammar School Magazine*, Vol. 26, No. 3, Dec. 1929.
pp. 80–1: 'Desert Idyll' ('A play in one bout').
pp. 82–4: 'Modern Poetry' (prose).

C. 11 *Swansea Grammar School Magazine*, Vol. 27, No. 1, Apr. 1930.
p. 13: 'Request to an obliging poet' (poem).
pp. 25–6: 'In borrowed plumes' (poem).

C. 12 *Swansea Grammar School Magazine*, Vol. 27, No. 2, July 1930.
p. 45: 'Orpheus' (poem).
pp. 54–6: 'The Films' (prose).
pp. 56–8: 'Mr William Shakespeare' (prose—with P. E.
Smart).

C. 13 *Swansea Grammar School Magazine*, Vol. 27, No. 3, Dec. 1930.
pp. 87–9: 'Children's Hour, or Why the B.B.C. Broke
Down' (prose).
p. 93: 'Captain Bigger's Isle' (poem).

C. 14   *Swansea Grammar School Magazine*, Vol. 28, No. 1, Apr. 1931.
pp. 139–40: 'Brember' (prose).
p. 140: 'Two Images' (poems, 10 lines and 9 lines).
p. 155: 'The Tub' (poem).
  'Two Images' was reprinted in *Adam*, Year 21, No. 238, 1953, p. 67.

C. 15   *Swansea Grammar School Magazine*, Vol. 28, No. 2, July 1931.
pp. 186–7: 'The Terrible Tale of Tom Tipplewhite' (poem).
pp. 191–6: 'The sincerest form of flattery' (prose and poetry).
p. 190: 'The callous stars' (poem).
p. 200: 'Two decorations' (poem).

C. 16   *Herald of Wales*, 9th Jan. 1932.
p. 7: 'The Poets of Swansea. Walter Savage Landor to James Chapman Woods' (article).

C. 17   *Herald of Wales*, 23rd Jan. 1932.
p. 6: 'Tragedy of Swansea's comic genius. The story of Llewelyn Prichard, author of Twm Shon Catti' (article).

C. 18   *Herald of Wales*, 20th Feb. 1932.
p. 4: 'Minor poets of old Swansea. James John Evans, C. D. Morgan, H. A. W. Rott, Carl Morgannwy, "E.E." of Caswell, and Thomas Hood' (article).

C. 19   *Herald of Wales*, 19th Mar. 1932.
p. 4: 'Minor Poets of Swansea. A study of Pierre Claire' (article).

C. 20   *Herald of Wales*, 23rd Apr. 1932.
p. 4: 'Verse of James Chapman Woods. A Critical Estimate. Swansea's greatest poet' (article).

C. 21   *Herald of Wales*, 25th June 1932.
p. 8: 'A Modern Poet of Gower' (Mr E. Howard Harris) (article).

C. 22   *Herald of Wales*, 5th Nov. 1932.
p. 6: 'A Baroness Journeys on to Gower. Lady Barham's Six Chapels. The Story of Paraclete. End of a Great Ministry' (article).

C. 23   *Swansea Grammar School Magazine*, Vol. 30, No. 2, July 1933.
pp. 64–5: 'Decline and Fall of Cassius Jones. A Cautionary Poem' (poem, 12 verses of 5, 4, 4, 6, 7, 5, 4, 4, 4, 5, 3, and 4 lines. Signed 'D.M.T. (O.B.)').

C. 24   *Herald of Wales*, 15th July 1933.
p. 1: 'Greek Play in a Garden' (poem, first line: 'A woman

wails her dead among the trees,'; 7 verses of 4, 8, 4, 4, 4, 4, and 4 lines).

This poem was reprinted in the programme of the Dylan Thomas memorial arranged by the Swansea Little Theatre at the Bishop Gore School on 17th Mar. 1954 (p. 3), with the following note: 'Dylan Thomas was an active member of Swansea Little Theatre and after seeing the "Electra" of Sophocles played in a garden at Sketty Green in 1933 he wrote this poem. . . .'

Reprinted again in *Quite Early One Morning*, 1954, pp. 177–8.

C. 25   *Adelphi*, Vol. 6, No. 6, Sept. 1933.
p. 398: poem—'No man believes who, when a star falls shot' (A. 1).

C. 26   *Sunday Referee*, 3rd Sept. 1933.
'Poets' Corner': poem—'That Sanity Be Kept' (A. 2).

C. 27   *Sunday Referee*, 29th Oct. 1933.
'Poets' Corner': poem—'The force that through the green fuse drives the flower' (A. 3).

C. 28   *Swansea Grammar School Magazine*, Vol. 30, No. 3, Dec. 1933.
pp. 137–9: 'Jarley's' (a short prose piece about a travelling waxworks).

C. 29   *Sunday Referee*, 7th Jan. 1934.
'Poets' Corner': 'Song' ('Love me, not as the dreaming nurses') (A. 4).

C. 30   *New English Weekly*, Vol. 4, No. 15, 25th Jan. 1934.
pp. 342–3: poem—'Out of the Pit' ('Within his head revolved a little world') (A. 5).

C. 31   *Sunday Referee*, 11th Feb. 1934.
'Poets' Corner': poem—'A process in the weather of the heart' (A. 6).

C. 32   *Adelphi*, Vol. 7, No. 6, Mar. 1934.
pp. 399–400: poem—'The Woman Speaks' ('No food suffices but the food of death') (A. 7).

C. 33   *Listener*, Vol. 11, No. 270, 14th Mar. 1934.
p. 462: poem—'Light breaks where no sun shines' (A. 8).

C. 34   *New English Weekly*, Vol. 4, No. 22, 15th Mar. 1934.
pp. 515–16: story—'After the Fair.'
This story was reprinted in *New World Writing*, 7th Mentor Selection, N.Y., 1955 (April), and first appeared in book form a month later in *Adventures in the Skin Trade* (see C. 194 and B. 27). Both these printings are identical to the original.

C. 35   *Sunday Referee*, 25th Mar. 1934.
    'Poets' Corner': poem—'Where once the waters of your face' (A. 9).

C. 36   *New Verse*, No. 8, Apr. 1934.
    pp. 11–12: poem—'Our eunuch dreams, all seedless in the light' (A. 10).

C. 37   *New Verse*, No. 9, June 1934.
    pp. 6–8: poem—'When once the twilight locks no longer' (A. 11).
    pp. 8–9: poem—'I see the boys of summer in their ruin' (A. 12).

C. 38   *New Stories* (Oxford), Vol. 1, No. 3, June|July 1934.
    pp. 194–8: story—'The Enemies.'
    This story was reprinted in *Yellow Jacket*, No. 1, Mar. 1939, pp. 32–7, and first appeared in book form in *The Map of Love* (B. 4).

C. 39   *New Verse*, No. 10, Aug. 1934.
    pp. 8–9: poem—'If I was [*sic*] tickled by the rub of love' (A. 13).

C. 40   *Adelphi*, Vol. 8, No. 6, Sept. 1934.
    pp. 418–20: reviews of *The Solitary Way* by William Soutar, *Squared Circle* by William Montgomerie, and *Thirty Pieces* by Sydney Salt.

C. 41   *Criterion*, Vol. 14, No. 54, Oct. 1934.
    pp. 27–8: poem—'From love's first fever to her plague, from the soft second' (A. 14).

C. 42   *New Verse*, No. 11, Oct. 1934.
    pp. 8–9: Answers to an Enquiry.
    This issue of *New Verse* was devoted to answers to six questions put to forty leading poets.   Thomas's contribution covers approx. 1½ pp.

C. 43   *Listener*, Vol. 12, No. 302, 24th Oct. 1934.
    p. 691: 'Poem in October' ('Especially when the October wind') (A. 15).

C. 44   *Sunday Referee*, 28th Oct. 1934.
    'Poets' Corner': poem—'Foster the light, nor veil the feeling [*sic*] moon' (1st version—A. 16).

C. 45   *New English Weekly*, Vol. 6, No. 6, 22nd Nov. 1934.
    pp. 132–4: story—'The End of the River.'
    A moving story about the last, childless member of an old and once vigorous family.   Not so far reprinted.

C. 46 *Adelphi*, Vol. 9, No. 3, Dec. 1934.
pp. 143–9: story—'The Tree.'
This story first appeared in book form in *The Map of Love* (B. 4) but with a number of alterations and deletions.

C. 47 *New Verse*, No. 12, Dec. 1934.
pp. 10–12: poem—'Half of the fellow father as he doubles' (A. 17).
pp. 19–20: 'Fey, Dollfuss, Vienna.'   Review of *Vienna* by Stephen Spender (signed 'D.M.T.').

C. 47a The *Bookman*, Christmas 1934.
p. 12 ('Art, Poetry & Criticism' Section): 'Individual and Collective'—reviews of *A Mad Lady's Garland* by Ruth Pitter, *Fuel* by Wilfrid Gibson, *The Noise of History* by John Lehmann, and *The Best Poems of 1934* ed. Thomas Moult.
(Thomas's name at the head of this article is mis-spelt 'Dylon Thomas.'

C. 48 *Adelphi*, Vol. 9, No. 4, Jan. 1935.
pp. 255–6: review of *Songs From Prison* by M. K. Gandhi.

C. 49 *Criterion*, Vol. 15, No. 55, Jan. 1935.
pp. 251–9: story—'The Visitor.'
This story first appeared in book form in *The Best Short Stories of 1935: English and American* (D. 2).   Later in *The Map of Love* (B. 4) but with a few small alterations and rearrangements and the name 'Millicent' changed to 'Rhianon.'

C. 50 *Adelphi*, Vol. 9, No. 5, Feb. 1935.
pp. 312–14: reviews of *Into the Light, and Other Poems* by Lyle Donaghy, *The Noise of History* by John Lehmann, and *A Mad Lady's Garland* by Ruth Pitter.
pp. 317–18: review of *Dictator in Freedom, Tract Four* by Alfred Hy. Haffenden.

C. 51 *Adelphi*, Vol. 10, No. 3, June 1935.
pp. 179–81: review of *The Poems of John Clare*, 2 vols., ed. J. W. Tibble.

C. 52 *Herald of Wales*, No. 6,746, 8th June 1935.
p. 1: poem—'Poet: 1935' ('See, on gravel paths under the harpstrung trees,') (A. 25).

C. 53 *Sunday Referee*, 11th Aug. 1935.
'Poets' Corner': 'Poem for Sunday' ('Incarnate devil in a talking snake,') (A. 26).

C. 54 *New Verse*, No. 16, Aug.–Sept. 1935.
pp. 2–5: 'A Poem in Three Parts' ('I, in my intricate image, stride on two levels,') (A. 27).

Opposite: COLLECTED POEMS—title-page of
Dent edition (B. 16 & 17)

DYLAN THOMAS

Collected Poems

1934–1952

LONDON

J. M. DENT & SONS LTD

C. 55   *Morning Post*, 24th Sept. 1935.
p. 14: 'New Thrillers'—reviews of *The House on the Roof* by
M. G. Eberhart, *Go Home, Unicorn* by Donald Macpherson,
Death in B. Minor by Jean Lilly, and *The Children of Light* by
Robert Curtis.

C. 56   *Adelphi*, Vol. 11, No. 1, Oct. 1935.
pp. 58–9: review of *A Comparison of Literatures* by R. D.
Jameson.

C. 57   *Scottish Bookman*, Vol. 1, No. 2, Oct. 1935.
p. (78): poem—'Do you not father me, nor the erected
arm' (A. 28).

C. 58   *Morning Post*, 11th Oct. 1935.
p. 15: 'Frequent, Gory and Grotesque'—reviews of *The
Hollow Man* by John Dickson Carr, *Mystery at Olympia* by John
Rhode, *Murder in College* by J. Y. Dane, and *Murder in Mid-
summer* by Mary M. Atwater.

C. 59   *Morning Post*, 15th Oct. 1935.
p. 16: 'Revolver, Sandbag, Hand-Grenade . . . '—reviews
of *The Stolen Boat-Train* by Douglas G. Browne, *Gun Business*
by Grierson Dickson, *The Milk Churn Murder* by Miles Burton,
and *Death Blew Out the Match* by Kathleen Moore Knight.

C. 60   *Programme* (Oxford), No. 9, 23rd Oct. 1935.
pp. (2)–(3): poem—'How soon the servant sun' (A. 30).
pp. (10)–(12): poem—'A grief ago' (A. 29).

C. 61   *Morning Post*, 25th Oct. 1935.
p. 15: 'A Choice of New Thrillers.   Meet Mr Nero Wolfe'
—reviews of *The League of Frightened Men* by Rex Stout,
Death on Deposit by Francis D. Grierson, and *The Case Against
Mrs Ames* by Arthur Somers Roche.

C. 62   *Morning Post*, 1st Nov. 1935.
p. 14: 'Two Thrillers'—reviews of *Beauty Vanishes* by
Dorothea Brande, and *Murder in Oils* by John Newton Chance.

C. 63   *Morning Post*, 5th Nov. 1935.
p. 14: 'Grand Goose Flesh Parade'—reviews of *A Century
of Horror*, ed. Dennis Wheatley, and *50 Years of Ghost Stories*.

C. 64   *Morning Post*, 15th Nov. 1935.
p. 6: 'Three New Thrillers'—reviews of *Danger at Cliff
House* by Cecil Freeman, *The Cases of Susan Dare* by Mignon G.
Eberhart, and *Death in the Wheelbarrow* by William Gore.

C. 65   *Morning Post*, 22nd Nov. 1935.
p. 14: 'Lord Peter Does Another Job.   Some of the Latest

Thrillers'—reviews of *Gaudy Night* by Dorothy L. Sayers, *The Red Window Murders* by Carter Dickson, *Heir Presumptive* by Henry Wade, and *Death's Juggler* by Carroll John Daly.

C. 66   *Morning Post*, 29th Nov. 1935.
p. 16: 'He Was Framed With a False Eye'—reviews of *The Case of the Counterfeit Eye* by Erle Stanley Gardner, *Not Proven* by Bruce Graeme, *The Garden Murder Case* by S. S. Van Dine, and *The Emerald Spider* by Gavin Holt.

C. 67   *Life and Letters Today*, Vol. 13, No. 2, Dec. 1935.
pp. 73–5: 'Poems for a Poem' ('Altarwise by owl-light in the half-way house'; 'Death is all metaphors, shape in one history;'; 'First there was the lamb on knocking knees'; 'What is the metre of the dictionary?'; 'And from the windy west came two-gunned Gabriel,'; 'Cartoon of slashes on the tide-traced crater,'; 'Now stamp the lord's prayer on a grain of rice,': A. 31–7).

C. 68   *New Verse*, No. 18, Dec. 1935.
pp. 15–17: 'Three Poems' ('The hand that signed the paper felled a city;'; 'Should lanterns shine, the holy face,'; 'I have longed to move away': A. 38–40).

C. 69   *Comment*, Vol. 1, No. 5, 4th Jan. 1936.
pp. 34–5: story—'The Dress.'
This story first appeared in book form in *The Map of Love* (B. 4).

C. 70   *Morning Post*, 7th Jan. 1936.
p. 15: 'Murders for the New Year. An Agatha Christie Triumph'—reviews of *The ABC Murders* by Agatha Christie, *Death in the Tunnel* by Miles Burton, and *Murder by Chance* by Peter Drax.

C. 71   *Morning Post*, 17th Jan. 1936.
p. 14: 'Dead Bodies, Live Villains. Another Triumph for Richard Hull'—reviews of *Vultures in the Sky* by Todd Downing, *Murder Isn't Easy* by Richard Hull, *Agents of the League* by Colin Davy, and *Cliffs of Sark*, by Gordon Valk.

C. 72   *Morning Post*, 31st Jan. 1936.
p. 14: 'Murder From Inside. Drunkards, Poisoners, Thick Ears'—reviews of *Cowardly Custard* by Baroness von Hutten, *The Nursing Home Murder* by Ngaio Marsh and H. Jellett, *The Strange Case of Harriet Hall* by Moray Dalton, and *Meet the Dragon* by David Hume.

C. 73   *Comment*, Vol. 1, No. 9, 1st Feb. 1936.
p. 66: poem—'Grief thief of time crawls off,' (A. 41).

C. 74 *Morning Post*, 7th Feb. 1936.
  p. 20: 'Patient Detection'—reviews of *The Loss of the Jane
  Vosper* by Freeman Wills Crofts, *Sandbar Sinister* by Phoebe
  Atwood Taylor, and *It Couldn't Be Murder* by Hugh Austin.

C. 75 *Morning Post*, 11th Feb. 1936.
  p. 16: 'The Week's Blood and Fun.   A Knowing Thriller'
  —reviews of *The Good Books* by R. Philmore, *The Puzzle of the
  Briar Pipe* by Stuart Palmer, *Reduction of Staff* by F. J. Whaley,
  and *Murder Without Mourners* by Sutherland Scott.

C. 76 *Caravel* (Majorca), Vol. 2, No. 5, Mar. 1936.
  p. (15): poem—'Hold hard, these ancient minutes in the
  cuckoo's month,' (A. 42).

C. 77 *Purpose*, Vol. 8, No. 2, Apr.–June 1936.
  pp. 102–3: poem—'Fine [*sic*] meat on bones that soon have
  none,' (A. 43).

C. 78 *Life and Letters Today*, Vol. 14, No. 3, Spring 1936.
  pp. 129–32: story—'The Lemon.'
     This story first appeared in book form, unchanged, in
  Adventures in the Skin Trade (B. 27).

C. 79 *Contemporary Poetry and Prose*, No. 1, May 1936.
  p. 2: poem—'This was the crucifixion on the mountain,'
  (A. 44).
  pp. 2–3: poem—'Foster the light, nor veil the manshaped
  moon,' (2nd version—A. 16).
  pp. 10–14: story—'The Burning Baby.'
     'The Burning Baby' first appeared in book form in *New
  Directions 1939* (D. 7); first appearance in a book under
  Thomas's authorship was in *The World I Breathe* (B. 5).   Same
  text in all cases.

C. 80 *Janus* (No. 2), May 1936.
  pp. 4–9: story—'The Horse's Ha.'
     This story first appeared in book form, unchanged, in
  Adventures in the Skin Trade (B. 27).

C. 81 *Criterion*, Vol. 15, No. 61, July 1936.
  pp. 614–22: story—'The Orchards.'
     This story first appeared in book form in *Welsh Short Stories*
  (D. 3).   Later it appeared in *The Map of Love* (B. 4), but here
  the name 'Peter' becomes 'Marlais' throughout and a few
  minor word-changes occur.   Reprinted in *Adventures in the
  Skin Trade* and *A Prospect of the Sea* (B. 27 and 28).   'Llareggub'
  is here first mentioned (para. 2).

C. 82   *Contemporary Poetry and Prose*, No. 3, July 1936.
p. 53: 'Two Poems Towards a Poem'—'From the oracular archives and the parchment,' (A. 45) and 'Let the tale's sailor from a Christian voyage' (A. 46).

C. 83   *New English Weekly*, Vol. 9, No. 14, 16th July 1936.
p. 270: 'Two Poems'—'Why east wind chills and south wind cools' (A. 47) and 'This bread I break was once the oat,' (A. 48).

C. 84   *New English Weekly*, Vol. 9, No. 16, 30th July 1936.
p. 310: poem—'Before we mothernaked fall' (A. 49).

C. 85   *Contemporary Poetry and Prose*, No. 4/5, Aug.–Sept. 1936.
pp. 95–100: story—'The School for Witches.'
This story first appeared in book form in *New Directions 1939* (D. 7); later in *The World I Breathe* (B. 5).   Same text in all cases.

C. 86   *New English Weekly*, Vol. 9, No. 17/20, 3rd Sept. 1936.
p. 328: poem—'Was there a time when dancers with their fiddles' (A. 50).

C. 87   *Transition*, No. 25, Fall 1936.
pp. 43–58: story—'The Mouse and the Woman.'
This story first appeared in book form, unchanged, in *The Map of Love* (B. 4).

C. 88   *Purpose*, Vol. 8, No. 4, Oct.–Dec. 1936.
pp. 230–1: poem—'Then was my neophyte,' (A. 58).
pp. 231–2: poem—'Today, this insect, and the world I breathe,' (A. 59).

C. 89   *Poetry* (Chicago), Vol. 49, No. 4, Jan. 1937.
p. 183: poem—'We lying by seasand, watching yellow' (A. 60).

C. 90   *Twentieth Century Verse*, No. 1, Jan. 1937.
p. (3): poem—'It is the sinners' dust-tongued bell claps me to churches' (A. 61).

C. 91   *Life and Letters Today*, Vol. 16, No. 7, Spring 1937.
pp. 65–70: story—'A Prospect of the Sea.'
This story first appeared in book form, unchanged, in *The World I Breathe* (B. 5).

C. 92   *Contemporary Poetry and Prose*, No. 9, Spring 1937.
pp. 18–26: story—'The Holy Six.'
This story first appeared in book form, unchanged, in *The World I Breathe* (B. 5).

C. 93   *Wales*, No. 1, Summer 1937.
        pp. 1–6: story—'Prologue to an Adventure.' (The title and
        first few lines also appeared on the front cover.)
        This story first appeared in book form in *The World I
        Breathe* (B. 5). Reprinted in *Adventures in the Skin Trade*
        (B. 27). Text unchanged.

C. 94   *Wales*, No. 3, Autumn 1937.
        pp. 116–23: story—'The Map of Love.'
        This story first appeared in book form in *The Map of Love*
        (B. 4), text unchanged.

C. 95   *New Verse*, No. 26/27 (Auden Double Number), Nov. 1937.
        p. 25: prose—(tribute to W. H. Auden, 13 lines).

C. 96   *Twentieth Century Verse*, No. 8, Jan.–Feb. 1938.
        pp. (3)–(4): 'Poem (for Caitlin)' ('I make this in a warring
        absence when') (A. 62).

C. 97   *Wales*, No. 4, Mar. 1938.
        p. 138: poem—'The spire cranes. Its statue is an aviary.'
        (A. 63).
        pp. 147–8: prose—'In the Direction of the Beginning.'
        This prose piece first appeared in book form in *New
        Directions 1938* (D. 5). Later in *Adventures in the Skin Trade*
        (B. 27).

C. 98   *New English Weekly*, Vol. 12, No. 22, 10th Mar. 1938.
        pp. 431–2: story—'A Visit to Grandpa's.'
        This story first appeared in book form in *Portrait of the
        Artist as a Young Dog* (B. 6).

C. 99   *New English Weekly*, Vol. 12, No. 23, 17th Mar. 1938.
        pp. 454–5: 'Recent Novels'—reviews of *Murphy* by Samuel
        Beckett, and *Life Along the Passaic River* by William Carlos
        Williams.

C. 100 *New English Weekly*, Vol. 13, No. 2, 21st Apr. 1938.
        pp. 34–5: 'Recent Novels'—reviews of *Epitaph for a Spy* by
        Eric Ambler, and *Not All Sleep* by Sheila Radice.

C. 101 *New English Weekly*, Vol. 13, No. 6, 19th May 1938.
        pp. 115–16: 'Recent Novels'—reviews of *Sinister Smith* by
        A. H. Atkins, *Arrogant Alibi* by C. Daly King, *Haven's End* by
        John P. Marquand, and *Their Eyes Were Watching God* by
        Norah Hurston.

C. 102 *Wales*, No. 5, Summer 1938.
        pp. 179–81: 'Poem (for Caitlin)' ('I make this in a warring
        absence when') (2nd version—A. 62).

G

C. 103   *Life and Letters Today*, Vol. 18, No. 12, Summer 1938.
p. 45: poem—'(In Memory of Ann Jones)' ('After the funeral, mule praises, brays,') (A. 64).

C. 104   *La Nouvelle Saison*, Vol. 1, No. 3, Paris, July 1938.
Contains French trans. of the poem 'The hand that signed the paper . . .', probably the first work of Thomas to appear in translation. (*See* A. 38.)

C. 105   *Poetry* (Chicago), Vol. 52, No. 5, Aug. 1938.
pp. 247–9: 'Four Poems'—'When all my five and country senses see,' (A. 67), 'O make me a mask and a wall to shut from your spies' (A. 66), 'Not from this anger, anticlimax after' (A. 65), and 'The spire cranes. Its statue is an aviary' (2nd version—A. 63).

C. 106   *New English Weekly*, Vol. 13, No. 17/21, 1st Sept. 1938.
p. 312: 'Recent Novels'—reviews of *The Trumpet Is Mine* by Cecil Lewis, *The Green Fool* by Patrick Kavanagh, and *Time Will Knit* by Fred Urquhart.

C. 107   *New English Weekly*, Vol. 13, No. 24, 22nd Sept. 1938.
p. 360: 'Taverns in General'—review of *Pub Survey* by George N. List.

C. 108   *Criterion*, Vol. 18, No. 70, Oct. 1938.
pp. 29–30: poem—'How shall my animal' (A. 68).

C. 109   *Life and Letters Today*, Vol. 19, No. 14, Oct. 1938.
pp. 76–95: story—'The Peaches.'
This story first appeared in book form in *Portrait of the Artist as a Young Dog* (B.6), but is there broken into more paragraphs (mostly for dialogue purposes) and has also one swear-word reduced to an abbreviation.

C. 110   *New English Weekly*, Vol. 14, No. 1, 13th Oct. 1938.
pp. 11–12: 'Recent Fiction'—reviews of *Monday Night* by Kay Boyle, *Last Stories* by Mary Butts, *War Paint* by F. V. Morley, and *Dolby Green* by Walter Brierley.

C. 111   *New English Weekly*, Vol. 14, No. 6, 17th Nov. 1938.
pp. 92–3: 'Recent Fiction'—reviews of *Apropos of Dolores* by H. G. Wells, *Free Land* by Rose Wilder Lane, *I Lost My Girlish Laughter* by Jane Allen, and *Port of Refuge* by Signe Toksvig.

C. 112   *Seven*, No. 3, Winter 1938.
p. 17: poems—'Her tombstone told when she died.' (A. 69), and 'I, the first named, am the ghost of this sir and christian friend' (A. 70).

C. 113 *Life and Letters Today*, Vol. 20, No. 16, Dec. 1938.
p. 42: 'Birthday Poem'—'Twenty-four years remind the tears of my eyes' (A. 71).

C. 114 *Voice of Scotland*, Vol. 1, No. 3, Dec. 1938–Feb. 1939.
p. 12: poem—'The tombstone told me when she died' (2nd version—A. 69).

C. 115 *Twentieth Century Verse*, No. 15/16, Feb. 1939.
p. 149: poem—'January 1939' ('Because the pleasure-bird whistles after the hot wires,') (A. 72).

C. 116 *New English Weekly*, Vol. 14, No. 17, 2nd Feb. 1939.
pp. 256–7: 'Dos Passos and Kafka'—reviews of *U.S.A.* by John Passos, and *America* by Franz Kafka.

C. 117 *Poetry* (London), No. 1, Feb. 1939.
pp. (26)–(27): 'Poem in the Ninth Month' ('A saint about to fall,') (A. 73).
There are also some notes on Thomas and his imitators in the 'First Letter' by the editor.

C. 118 *Wales*, No. 6/7, Mar. 1939.
p. 196: 2 poems—'On no work of words . . . ' (A. 74), and 'Once it was the colour of saying' (A. 75).

C. 119 *Poetry* (London), No. 2, Apr. 1939.
p. (25): poem—'"If my head hurt a hair's foot"' (A. 76).
p. (31): letter to the editor congratulating him on the magazine (7 lines).

C. 120 *Seven*, No. 4, Spring 1939.
pp. 45–8: story—'An Adventure from a Work in Progress.'
This story first appeared in book form in *Adventures in the Skin Trade* (B. 27).

C. 121 *Yellowjacket*, Vol. 1, No. 2, May 1939.
pp. 60–3: story—'The True Story.'
pp. 64–7: story—'The Vest.'
Both these stories appeared for the first time in book form in *Adventures in the Skin Trade* (B. 27).

C. 122 *New English Weekly*, Vol. 15, No. 5, 18th May 1939.
pp. 79–80: 'Recent Fiction'—reviews of *At Swim-Two-Birds* by Flann O'Brien, *Over the Mountain* by Ruthven Todd, and *Journeyman* by Erskine Caldwell.

C. 123 *Life and Letters Today*, Vol. 22, No. 23, July 1939.
pp. 66–80: story—'Old Garbo.'
This story first appeared in book form in *Portrait of the Artist as a Young Dog* (B. 6), but with some 300 words added at the beginning and with a few small alterations.

C. 124   *Life and Letters Today*, Vol. 22, No. 25, Sept. 1939.
pp. 415–25: story—'Extraordinary Little Cough.'
This story first appeared in book form in *Portrait of the Artist as a Young Dog* (B. 6), but with dialogue broken into more paragraphs.

C. 125   *Seven*, No. 6, Autumn 1939.
p. 5: poem—'To Others Than You' ('Friend by enemy I call you out.') (A. 77).
p. 6: poem—'Paper and Sticks' (A. 78).
p. 7: poem—'When I woke, the town spoke' (A. 79).

C. 126   *Life and Letters Today*, Vol. 23, No. 26, Oct. 1939.
pp. 66–8: 'Poem (to Caitlin)' ('Unluckily for a death') (A. 80—first version).

C. 127   *Wales*, No. 10, Oct. 1939.
pp. 255–60: story—'Just Like Little Dogs.'
This story first appeared in book form in *Portrait of the Artist as a Young Dog* (B. 6), but with the names of the girls in 'Tom's' narrative switched at the end, throwing rather a different light on the denouement.   There are also a few minor word changes and more paragraphing.

C. 128   *Life and Letters Today*, Vol. 23, No. 27, Dec. 1939.
pp. 326–39: story—'The Fight.'
This story first appeared in book form in *Portrait of the Artist as a Young Dog* (B. 6), but with 'Mr Daniels' altered to 'Mr Samuels' and a few other minor revisions.

C. 129   *New English Weekly*, Vol. 16, No. 9, 14th Dec. 1939.
pp. 133–5: 'Novels and Novelists'—reviews of *Night of the Poor* by Frederic Prokosch, *Here Lies* by Dorothy Parker, and *A Villa in Sicily* by Georg Kaiser.

C. 130   *Seven*, No. 7, Christmas 1939.
pp. 4–11: story—'Patricia, Edith, and Arnold.'
This story first appeared in book form in *Portrait of the Artist as a Young Dog* (B. 6), but with a few alterations in spacing and punctuation.

C. 131   *Life and Letters Today*, Vol. 24, No. 31, Mar. 1940 (Welsh Number).
pp. 274–5: poem—'Once below a time' (A. 81).

C. 132   *Horizon*, Vol. 1, No. 5, May 1940.
pp. 318–19: poem—'There was a saviour' (A. 82).

C. 133   *Cambridge Front* (No. 1), Summer 1940.
pp. 8–9: poem—'The Countryman's Return' ('Embracing low-falutin') (A. 83).

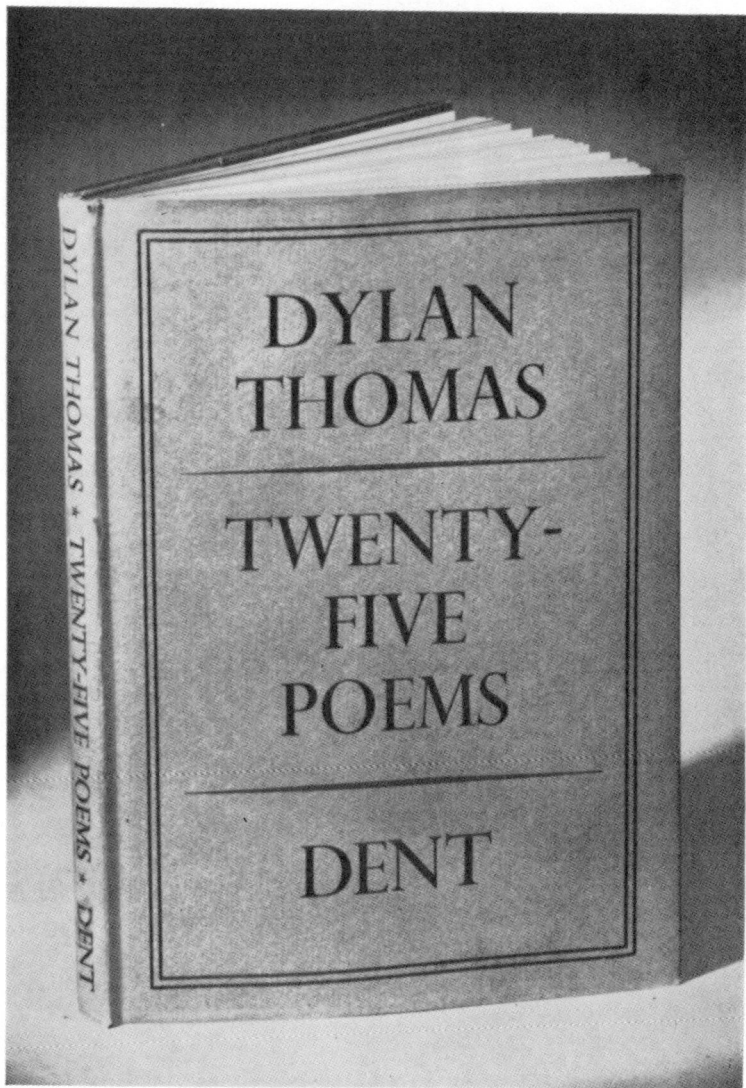

TWENTY-FIVE POEMS, first edition—grey dust-wrapper (B. 3)

This magazine is not in fact numbered and was presumably not intended to be the first of a series, though another number appeared in 1941. The editor was George Scurfield, assisted by Mark Holloway and Nicholas Moore. Only a few hundred copies were printed (in Cambridge).

C. 134   *Life and Letters Today*, Vol. 27, No. 39, Nov. 1940.
pp. 124–6: poem—'Into her lying down head' (A. 84—first version).

C. 135   *Horizon*, Vol. 3, No. 13, Jan. 1941.
pp. 12–13: poem—'Deaths and Entrances' ('On almost the incendiary eve') (A. 85).

C. 136   *Poetry* (London), No. 4, 15th Jan. 1941.
p. 91: poem—'On a Wedding Anniversary' ('At last, in a wrong rain,') (A. 86—first version).

C. 137   *Poetry* (London), No. 6, May–June 1941.
pp. 186–7: poem—'Love in the Asylum' ('A stranger has come') (A. 87).

C. 138   *Horizon*, Vol. 4, No. 19, July 1941.
pp. 9012: poem—'Ballad of the Long-legged Bait' ('The bows glided down, and the coast') (A. 88).

C. 139   *Life and Letters Today*, Vol. 30, No. 48, Aug. 1941.
p. 116: poem—'Among Those Killed in the Dawn Raid Was a Man Aged a Hundred' ('When the morning was waking over the war') (A. 89).

C. 140   *Life and Letters Today*, Vol. 31, No. 50, Oct. 1941.
pp. 41–2: poem—'The hunchback in the park' (A. 90).
pp. 42–3: poem—'The Marriage of a Virgin.' ('Waking alone in a multitude of loves . . . ') (A. 91).

C. 141   *Horizon*, Vol. 6, No. 31, July 1942.
p. 6: poem—'Request to Leda' (Not your winged lust but his must now change suit') (A. 92).

C. 142   *Fontaine* (Alger) No. 25, Nov.–Dec. 1942.
Translations into French by Hélène Bokanowski, of three poems:
pp. 544–5: 'The force that through the green fuse drives the flower' (A. 3).
pp. 546–7: 'Light breaks where no sun shines' (A. 8).
pp. 547–8: 'This was the crucifixion on the mountain,' (A. 44).

C. 143   *Listener*, Vol. 29, No. 737, 25th Feb. 1943.
pp. 246–7: prose—'Reminiscences of Childhood.'

This is the first version of this prose piece. It was re-printed in 1954 elsewhere with drawings by Mervyn Peake (*see* C. 191), and first appeared in book form in *Quite Early One Morning* (B. 23), together with the second version (— English edition only: American edition contains only the second version).

C. 144   *Wales*, New Series No. 2, Autumn 1943.
          pp. 76–8: verse—'Our Country.'
          This is a free verse commentary by Thomas for the first two reels of a five-reeler documentary film made by John Eldridge and J. Jago, Strand Film Co., for the Ministry of Information.   It first appeared in book form in the American edition of *Quite Early One Morning* (B. 24).

C. 145   *Fontaine* (Alger) No. 37/40, 1944.
          pp. 441–3: translation into French by Hélène Bokanowski and Armand Guibert of the poem—'In Memory of Ann Jones' (A. 64).

C. 146   *Our Time*, Vol. 3, No. 10, May 1944.
          p. 10: poem—'Ceremony After a Fire Raid' ('Myselves | The grievers | grieve |' . . .) (A. 93).

C. 147   *Poetry* (London), No. 9, 1944.
          p. 34: two poems—'Last night I dived my beggar arm' (A. 94) and 'Your breath was shed' (A. 95).

C. 148   *Horizon*, Vol. 11, No. 61, Jan. 1945.
          pp. 8–13: poem—'Vision and Prayer' ('Who | are you | who is born |' . . .) (A. 96).
          p. 14: poem—'Holy Spring' ('O | Out of a bed of love |' . . .) (A. 97).

C. 149   *Horizon*, Vol. 11, No. 62, Feb. 1945.
          pp. 82–3: 'Poem in October' ('It was my thirtieth year to heaven') (A. 98).

C. 150   *New Republic*, Vol. 112, No. 20, 14th May 1945 (No. 1589).
          p. 675: poem—'A Refusal to Mourn the Death, by Fire, of a Child in London' ('Never until the mankind making') (A. 99).

C. 151   *Life and Letters Today*, Vol. 45, No. 94, June 1945.
          p. 155: poem—'Lie Still, Sleep Becalmed' (A. 100).

C. 152   *Life and Letters Today*, Vol. 46, No. 95, July 1945.
          pp. 28–9: poem—'This side of the truth,' (A. 101).
          p. 29: poem—'The Conversation of Prayers' (first printing but second version—*see* A. 102).

C. 153   *Poetry* (Chicago), Vol. 66, July 1945.
pp. 175–80: poem—'A Winter's Tale' ('It is a winter's tale') (A. 103).

C. 154   *New Republic*, Vol. 113, No. 3, 16th July 1945 (No. 1598).
p. 76: poem—'The Conversation of Prayers' (second printing but the only printing of the first version—*see* A. 102).

C. 155   *Horizon*, Vol. 12, No. 70, Oct. 1945.
pp. (221)–222: poem—'Fern Hill' ('Now as I was young and easy under the apple boughs') (A. 104).
Also contains 'A Refusal to Mourn . . . ', but this is not the first printing—*see* C. 150.

C. 156   *Life and Letters Today*, Vol. 47, No. 98, Oct. 1945.
p. 31: poem—'In my craft or sullen art' (A. 105).

C. 157   *Listener*, Vol. 34, No. 884, 20th Dec. 1945.
pp. 734–5: prose—'Memories of Christmas.'
This prose piece first appeared in book form in *Quite Early One Morning* (English edition—B. 23).

C. 158   *Horizon*, Vol. 14, No. 81, Sept. 1946.
pp. 173–5: prose—answers to 'Questionnaire: The Cost of Letters.'
Thomas's answers to this questionnaire, together with those of the other authors who contributed to it in *Horizon*, appeared for the first time in book form in *Ideas and Places* by Cyril Connolly (D. 20).

C. 159   *Wales*, No. 23 (Vol. 6, No. 3), Autumn 1946.
pp. 83–6: prose—'Quite Early One Morning.'
This prose piece first appeared in book form in the book *Quite Early One Morning* (B. 23) but with some of the names in the poem at the end changed.   Both versions were originally broadcast, the first in 1945 and the second in 1953 (*see* 'Notes' in B. 23).

C. 160   *Listener*, Vol. 36, No. 927, 17th Oct. 1946.
p. 508: prose—'How to Begin a Story.'
First published in book form in *Quite Early One Morning* (B. 23).

C. 161   *Listener*, Vol. 36, No. 930, 7th Nov. 1946.
pp. 634–5: prose—'Holiday Memory.'
First published in book form in *Quite Early One Morning* (B. 23).

C. 162   *Listener*, Vol. 37, No. 938, 2nd Jan. 1947.
pp. 28–9: prose—'The Crumbs of One Man's Year.'

First published in book form in *Quite Early One Morning* (B. 23).

C. 163   *Horizon*, Vol. 16, No. 96, Dec. 1947.
pp. 302–5: poem—'In Country Sleep' ('Never and never, my girl riding far and near') (A. 106).

C. 164   *Picture Post*, Vol. 37, No. 13, 27th Dec. 1947.
p. 26: prose—'Conversation About Christmas.'
The first appearance in 'book' form of this piece was the separate edition (in wrappers) printed 'for the friends of J. Laughlin and New Directions' at Christmas 1954 (B. 26), though this was never actually offered for sale. The piece forms the middle section of 'A Child's Christmas in Wales' (C. 170) which first appeared in book form in 1954 (*see* B. 24), but the first appearance in book form of the identical *Picture Post* text was in *A Prospect of the Sea* (B. 28), i.e. first *published* appearance in book form.

C. 165   *Listener*, Vol. 40, No. 1019, 5th Aug. 1948.
p. 205: prose—'The English Festival of Spoken Poetry.'
This piece first appeared in book form in *Quite Early One Morning* (B. 23) but with about seven extra lines at the end.

C. 166   *Botteghe Oscure*, No. 4 (Rome), Dec. 1949.
pp. 397–9: poem—'Over Sir John's Hill' (A. 107).

C. 167   *Circus*, No. 1, Apr. 1950.
pp. 7–12: prose—'How to Be a Poet (1).'
This piece, with the second part (C. 168), first appeared in book form in *Quite Early One Morning*, American edition (B. 24), but there without the first two paragraphs and without the 'Thank you' at end. With the exception of 'An editor,' which replaced 'Your editor' at the opening, the identical 'Circus' text first appeared in book form in *A Prospect of the Sea* (B. 28). The book form versions do not include the illustrations by Ronald Searle which appeared in *Circus*.

C. 168   *Circus*, No. 2, May 1950.
pp. 5–8: prose—'How to Be a Poet (2).'
Book form: *see* C. 167. This part runs from 'If this were the twenties . . . ' to the end.

C. 169   *Botteghe Oscure*, No. 6 (Rome), Nov. 1950.
pp. 335–7: poem—'In the White Giant's Thigh' ('Through throats where many rivers meet . . . ' (A. 108), followed by a note on the poem by the author (pp. 337–8).

C. 170   *Harper's Bazaar*, No. 2869, Dec. 1950. (American edition only.)

pp. 86–7, etc.: prose—'A Child's Memories of Christmas in Wales.'

This prose piece consists of an amalgamation of 'Memories of Christmas' (C. 157) and 'Conversation about Christmas' (C. 164). See *Quite Early One Morning*, American edition (B. 24), which contains first printing in book form thus.

C. 171   *Atlantic Monthly*, Vol. 188, July 1951.

pp. 46–9: prose—'How to Be a Poet.'

This is, apart from the first paragraph which is here omitted, the same version as appeared in the two issues of *Circus* (C. 167 and 168), but this printing represents the first appearance of the two parts conjoined into a consecutive whole. First appearance in book form: *see* C. 167.

C. 172   *Botteghe Oscure*, No. 8 (Rome), Nov. 1951.

p. 208: poem—'Do Not Go Gentle into That Good Night' (A. 109).

pp. 209–10: poem—'Lament' ('When I was a windy boy and a bit') (A. 110—first version).

C. 173   *World Review*, New Series, No. 32, Oct. 1951.

pp. 66–7: 'Poem on His Birthday' ('In the mustardseed sun,') (A. 111—first version).

C. 174   *Observer*, Sunday, 16th Dec. 1951.

'Flamboyants all the Way'—review of *Light on a Dark Horse* by Roy Campbell. Approx. 500 words.

C. 175   *Botteghe Oscure*, No. 9 (Rome), Apr. 1952.

pp. 134–53: prose and verse—'Llareggub (A Piece for Radio Perhaps).'

This forms the first half (to about p. 38 of the English edition) of what was to become *Under Milk Wood*, though in the book a few alterations occur, particularly towards the end of the periodical version.

pp. 154–5 contain a note by the author on the plan of the whole piece.

C. 176   *Observer*, Sunday, 6th July 1952.

'Blithe Spirits'—review of *The Palm-wine Drinkard* by Amos Tutuola. Approx. 500 words.

C. 177   *World Review*, New Series, No. 44, Oct. 1952.

pp. 41–5: story—'The Followers,' with three line-drawings by an unnamed artist.

This story first appeared in book form in *Adventures in the Skin Trade* (B. 27), though without the illustrations.

C. 178   *Listener*, Vol. 48, No. 1236, 6th Nov. 1952.
p. 773: poem—'Prologue' ('This day winding down now')
(A. 112).

C. 179   *New World Writing*, 2nd Mentor Selection, New York, Nov. 1952.
pp. 158–89: prose—'Adventures in the Skin Trade.'
This represents the first printing of the first two-thirds of the unfinished novel that bears the same title. The whole piece (C. 179, plus C. 180) first appeared in book form in *Adventures in the Skin Trade* (B. 27), in which this two-thirds runs from pp. 3–56.

C. 180   *New World Writing*, 3rd Mentor Selection, New York, May 1953.
pp. 192–207: prose—'Four Lost Souls.'
This represents the last third of the unfinished novel *Adventures in the Skin Trade* (B. 27), in which pp. 56–82 contain this section of the whole, constituting the first appearance in book form. (*See* C. 179.)

C. 181   *Listener*, Vol. 50, No. 1281, 17th Sept. 1953.
pp. 458–60: 'A Story,' with a drawing by Cecil Keeling.
This story, originally a television broadcast from London on 10th Aug. 1953, first appeared in book form in *Quite Early One Morning*, American edition (B. 24), though without the drawing.

C. 182   *Books*, The Journal of the National Book League, No. 282, Dec. 1953.
pp. 114–15: two letters embodied in an article 'Dylan Thomas' by E. F. Bozman.
Part of one of these letters was reprinted in *Adam*, No. 238 (C. 183).

C. 183   *Adam*, Year 21, No. 238 (Dylan Thomas Memorial Number), '1953.'
This issue contains, apart from the many essays about Thomas, reprints of poems from Thomas's school magazine, a portion of 'Adventure in the Skin Trade' appearing here for the first time in England, extracts from letters and numerous minor items. Contributors include Igor Stravinsky, Augustus John, Edith Sitwell, Pamela Hansford Johnson, John Davenport, George Barker, Runia Sheila MacLeod, Glyn Jones, Roy Campbell, Stephen Spender, and many others.

C. 184   *Encounter*, No. 4 (Vol. 2, No. 1), Jan. 1954.
         pp. 13–16: 'Dylan Thomas: Memories and Appreciations'—
         IV, Marjorie Adix.
             This 'appreciation' includes an apparently verbatim
         account of an interview with Thomas at the University of
         Utah in spring 1953.

C. 185   *Mademoiselle*, Vol. 38, No. 4, Feb. 1954.
         pp. 110–22: 'Under Milk Wood,' with photographs of
         Laugharne by Rollie McKenna, contd. pp. 144–56.
             First complete printing.   Preceded by 'Dylan Thomas and
         His Village' by John Malcolm Brinnin, pp. 108–9, illus.

C. 186   *Observer*, Sunday, 7th Feb. 1954.
         pp. 10–11: 'Under Milk Wood,' with drawings by John
         Minton.   Part I of an abridged version preceding the book
         by a few weeks (*see* B. 21 and C. 187).

C. 187   *Observer*, Sunday, 14th Feb. 1954.
         pp. 10–11: 'Under Milk Wood.'   Part II and last part of
         this abridgement (*see* C. 186).

C. 188   *Dock Leaves* (Pembroke Dock, Wales), Vol. 5, No. 13,
         Spring 1954.   ('A Dylan Thomas Number.')
             Articles on Thomas throughout this number contain
         snippets of original material such as quoted fragments of con-
         versation, etc.   Contributors include Aneirin Talfan Davies,
         Henry Treece, and others.

C. 189   *Listener*, Vol. 51, No. 1312, 22nd Apr. 1954.
         pp. 692–3: prose—'A Visit to America.'
             This prose piece, originally broadcast on 30th Mar. 1954,
         first appeared in book form in *Quite Early One Morning* (B. 23).

C. 190   *Botteghe Oscure*, No. 13 (Rome), Apr. 1953.
         pp. 93–102: three letters to the editor (Marguerite Caetani)
         concerning some promised contributions.

C. 191   *Encounter*, No. 10 (Vol. 3, No. 1), July 1954.
         pp. 3–7: prose—'Reminiscences of Childhood,' with draw-
         ings by Mervyn Peake.
             This is a reprint of the first version of this prose piece (*see*
         C. 143), but is its first appearance with illustrations.

C. 192   *Vogue*, Vol. 110, No. 1808, Nov. 1954.
         pp. 106–7, 166, and 170: prose—'Return Journey.'
             This is the first printing of this broadcast, though it was
         originally broadcast seven years earlier (15th June 1947) and
         repeated six times.   The piece first appeared in book form in
         Quite Early One Morning (B. 23) about a week later.

C. 193   *Encounter*, No. 14 (Vol. 3, No. 5), Nov. 1954.
pp. 23–6: broadcast discussion: 'On Poetry.'
    This is (by four days) the first printing of this broadcast of 18th June 1946, but it is also, as yet, the only truly complete printing since it includes the words of the other two participants in the discussion—James Stephens and Gerald Bullett. The first book form version, *Quite Early One Morning* (B. 23), has only Thomas's words—and these are slightly cut in places for the sake of consecutive prose.

C. 194   *New World Writing*, 7th Mentor Selection, New York, Apr. 1955.
pp. 128–40: 'Seven Letters to Oscar Williams,' with a portrait in colour of Thomas by Gene Derwood, and facsimiles of part of two of the letters. Followed by 'After the Fair' and 'The True Story'—these last, however, being reprints.

C. 195   *Encounter*, No. 29 (Vol. 6, No. 2), Feb. 1956.
pp. 30–1: poem—'Elegy' ('Too proud to die, broken and blind he died').
    First complete printing of Thomas's last, unfinished poem, here resolved and co-ordinated by Vernon Watkins from the quantity of manuscript material towards the poem which Thomas left. Followed by a note, p. 31.

C. 196   *Poetry London–New York*, Vol. I, No. 1, Mar.–Apr. 1956.
p. 12: two poems—'Last night I dived my beggar arm' and 'Your breath was shed', the first of these being here correctly printed for the first time (*see* A. 95).
Also in this number are appreciations of Thomas by Lawrence Durrell and Roy Campbell (pp. 34–6), and a review, by the editor (Tambimuttu), of Brinnin's *Dylan Thomas in America* (pp. 42–8).

DYLAN THOMAS

PORTRÆT
AF KUNSTNEREN SOM
HVALP

KØBENHAVN

GYLDENDAL

1955

PORTRAIT OF THE ARTIST AS A YOUNG DOG—title-page of Danish edition (E. 7)

Section D

Contributions by Dylan Thomas to Books

Note

Thomas did not wittingly contribute, in the usual sense of the word, to any book except *Folios of New Writing* (D. 9). The remainder of this section is comprised of books, other than books *by* Thomas, containing first printings in book form of individual writings.

New Directions in Prose and Poetry, though strictly an annual periodical and therefore liable for inclusion in *Section C*, is rather classified here as a 'book,' because its very appearance makes it so, I am sure, in the eyes of the majority. I have applied this criterion, as will be seen, in other cases; the measuring-rod has been throughout the binding style— 'periodicals' issued in cloth boards being treated as 'books,' and those in wrappers as 'periodicals.'

D. 1   *The Year's Poetry: A Representative Selection*, compiled by Denys Kilham Roberts, Gerald Gould, and John Lehmann. London, John Lane The Bodley Head, 1934.
pp. 133–4: poem—'Light' ('Light breaks where no sun shines'). First appearance in book form not only of this poem but also almost certainly of any work by Thomas. Published on 4th Dec. 1934, thus preceding *18 POEMS* by about two weeks (*see* A. 8).

D. 2   *The Best Short Stories of 1935: English and American*, ed. Edward O'Brien. London, Jonathan Cape, 1935.
pp. 206–14: story—'The Visitor.' First printing in book form, and only printing in book form with the original 'Millicent' throughout (later altered to 'Rhianon'). *See* C. 49.

D. 3   *Welsh Short Stories* (ed. the publishers, anonymously). London, Faber & Faber, 1937.
pp. 416–29: story—'The Orchards.' First printing in book

form, preceding *The Faber Book of Modern Stories* (ed. Elizabeth Bowen) by three weeks, after which, with a few other minor alterations, the name 'Peter' becomes 'Marlais'—i.e. in *The Map of Love*, et seq. (*see* C. 81).

D. 4   *The Year's Poetry 1937*, compiled by Denys Kilham Roberts and Geoffrey Grigson. London, John Lane The Bodley Head, 1937.
pp. 132–4: two poems—'We lying by seasand, . . . ' and 'It is the sinners' dust-tongued bell . . . '.   First printing in book form (*see* A. 60 and 61).

D. 5   *New Directions in Prose and Poetry*, 1938, ed. James Laughlin IV.   Norfolk, Conn., New Directions, 1938.
Contains the first printing in book form of three poems and a prose piece (pages unnumbered): 'In Memory of Ann Jones' ('After the funeral, . . . ') (A. 64).
'How shall my animal' (A. 68).
'I make this in a warring absence . . . ' (A. 62).
'In the Direction of the Beginning' (prose—*see* C. 97).

D. 6   *New Verse: An Anthology*, compiled by Geoffrey Grigson. London, Faber & Faber, 1939.
pp. 145–6: poem—'If I was tickled by the rub of love'. First and only printing in book form of this 'was' version (A. 13).

D. 7   *New Directions in Prose and Poetry 1939*, ed. James Laughlin IV.   Norfolk, Conn., New Directions, 1939.
Contains three first appearances in book form:
pp. 79–85: prose—'The Burning Baby.'   *See* C. 79.
pp. 86–93: prose—'The School for Witches.'   *See* C. 85.
p. 94: poem—'Her [*sic*] tombstone told when she died' (A. 69).

D. 8   *New Poems 1940*, ed. Oscar Williams.   New York, Yardstick Press, 1941.
pp. 214–24: various poems one of which appears here for the first time in book form, viz. 'Into her lying down head' (first version—*see* A. 84).

D. 9   *Folios of New Writing* (No. 4), Autumn 1941, ed. John Lehmann.   London, The Hogarth Press, 1941.
pp. 19–27: prose—'A Fine Beginning.'
This is the first printing of this piece in any form, and is described in the notes 'About the Contributors' as the 'first section of a longer work of prose fiction in preparation.' In fact it comprises the first half of Part I of 'Adventures in

the Skin Trade,' which first appeared in *New World Writing*, 2nd Mentor Selection, New York, 1952 (*see* C. 179).

D. 10   *Poetry in Wartime*, ed. M. J. Tambimuttu.   London, Faber & Faber, 1942.
pp. 169–70: poem—'Deaths and Entrances' ('On almost the incendiary eve') (A. 85).
pp. 170–1: poem—'On a Wedding Anniversary' ('At last, in a wrong rain,') (A. 86—first version).
First appearance in book form of both poems.

D. 11   *New Poems 1942*, ed. Oscar Williams.   Mount Vernon, N.Y., Peter Pauper Press, 1942.
pp. 227–41: five poems of which the following four appear here for the first time in book form:
'Ballad of the Long-legged Bait' ('The bows glided down, . . . ') (A. 88).
'The Hunchback in the Park' (A. 90).
'There was a saviour' (A. 82).
'The Marriage of a Virgin' ('Waking alone . . . ') (A. 91).

D. 12   *The War Poets: An Anthology of the War Poetry of the 20th Century*, ed. Oscar Williams.   New York, The John Day Co., 1945.
Contains three poems of which two appear here for the first time in book form, viz:
pp. 432–3: 'Holy Spring' ('O | Out of a bed of love | . . . ') (A. 97).
pp. 433–5: 'Ceremony After a Fire Raid' ('Myselves | the grievers | grieve | . . . ') (A. 93).

D. 13   *War and the Poet*, ed. Richard Eberhart and Selden Rodman. New York, The Devin-Adair Co., 1945.
pp. 200–1: poem—'A Refusal to Mourn the Death, by Fire, of a Child in London' ('Never until the mankind making') (A. 99).   First appearance in book form.

D. 14   *Little Reviews Anthology 1946*, ed. Denys Val Baker.   London, Eyre & Spottiswoode, 1946 (published on 29th Nov.).
pp. 89–91: 'Poem in October' ('It was my thirtieth year to heaven').   First printing in book form of the earlier version of this poem, though the later version had appeared in *Deaths and Entrances* in February the same year.   In 1947 the first version appeared again elsewhere (*see* A. 98).

D. 15   *Living Writers*, ed. G. H. Phelps.   London, The Sylvan Press, 1947.
pp. 116–27: prose—'Walter de la Mare.'
This book, consisting of a collection of twelve broadcast

talks, represents the first printing in any form of this prose piece.   The talk was reprinted in *Quite Early One Morning* (B. 23 and 24) entitled 'Walter de la Mare as a Prose Writer.'

D. 16   *First Time in America: A Selection of Poems Never Before Published in the U.S.A.*, ed. John Arlott.   New York, Duell, Sloane & Pearce, 1948.

pp. 181–2: two poems—'Last night I dived my beggar arm' and 'Your breath was shed' (A. 94 and A. 95).

First printing in book form of both poems, neither of which has appeared as yet in any book under Thomas's authorship.

D. 16a   *Poets at Work.   Essays Based on the Modern Poetry Collection at the Lockwood Memorial Library, University of Buffalo*, by Rudolf Arnheim, W. H. Auden, Karl Shapiro, and Donald A. Stauffer, Introduction by Charles D. Abbott.   New York, Harcourt Brace & Co., 1948.

p. 164: facsimile of Thomas's work-sheet of verses 52 and 53 of the 'Ballad of the Long-legged Bait,' showing various alterations (see A. 88).   A brief comment on these alterations, by W. H. Auden, appears on pp. 178–9.

D. 17   *Dylan Thomas, 'Dog Among the Fairies,'* by Henry Treece. London, Lindsay Drummond, 1949.

pp. 149–50: letter—'The Poet Answers a Critic' (as Appendix II).   First printing.   Comprising Thomas's comments on Edith Sitwell's review of *Twenty-Five Poems* in the *Sunday Times* of 15th Nov. 1936, p. 9.

There are also in this book several extracts from letters of Thomas to the author.   Several poems are also quoted for the first time in book form but none of them wholly (e.g. 'Request to Leda' on p. 116, verses 1 and 3).   12 lines of the 'Answers to an Enquiry' from *New Verse* (C. 42) appear on p. 39.

D. 18   *Little Reviews Anthology 1949*, ed. Denys Val Baker.   London, Methuen, 1949.

pp. (68)–71: poem—'In Country Sleep' ('Never and never, my girl riding far and near') (A. 106).

First printing in book form.

D. 19   *A Little Treasury of British Poetry: The Chief Poets from 1500 to 1950*, ed. Oscar Williams.   New York, Charles Scribner's Sons, 1951.

pp. 815–42: fourteen poems of which the two following appear here for the first time in book form:

'Over Sir John's Hill' (A. 107).

'In the White Giant's Thigh' ('Through throats where many rivers meet . . . ') (A. 108).

D. 20 *Ideas and Places*, by Cyril Connolly. London, Weidenfeld & Nicolson, 1953.

pp. 121–3: prose—answers to a questionnaire: 'The Cost of Letters.' First appearance in book form. The complete set of answers, originally in *Horizon* (C. 158), is here reprinted, pp. 79–126.

D. 21 *Fifth Annual Report to the Fellows of the Pierpont Morgan Library*, by Frederic B. Adams, Jr., New York, Nov. 1954, privately printed.

pp. 57–8: first appearance in any form of part of Thomas's last poem, 'Too proud to die, broken and blind he died'. *See* A. 113 for further details.

D. 22 *Dylan Thomas in America: An Intimate Journal*, by John Malcolm Brinnin, with photographs. An Atlantic Monthly Press Book; Boston, Little, Brown & Co., 1955.

Contains a hitherto unpublished version of part of Thomas's last poem (*see* A. 113), and also a number of letters.

H

Translations of Books
by Dylan Thomas

French

(Portrait of the Artist as a Young Dog)

E. 1 *Portrait de l'Artiste en Jeune Chien*, trans. Francis Dufau-
Labeyrie. Paris, Éditions de Minuit, Oct. 1947, 264 pp.,
sewn, 390 francs. '100 exemplaires sur papier Alfa-
Mousse des Papeteries de Navarre et 3,000 exemplaires
ordinaires.'

German

(Deaths and Entrances)

E. 2 *Tode und Tore*, trans. R. P. Becker. Heidelberg, Drei
Brücken Verlag, 1952, 91 pp., cloth, DM 8.80.
The edition consisted of 2,000 copies, the poems appearing
in English and German.

(Under Milk Wood)

E. 3 *Unter dem Milchwald*, trans. Erich Fried. Heidelberg, Drei
Brücken Verlag, 1954, 88 pp. Cloth: DM 8.80; boards,
DM 6.80.
The edition consisted of 3,000 copies.

Italian

(Poems)

E. 4 *Poesie*, trans., with introduction and notes, Roberto Sanesi.
Parma, Ugo Guanda, 1954, 204 pp., Lire 1,200. *Containing
the following poems:* I see the boys of summer—The force that
through the green fuse—My hero bares his nerves—Where
once the waters of your face—Especially when the October

wind—In the beginning—Light breaks where no sun shines—
I dreamed my genesis—All all and all the dry worlds lever—I,
in my intricate image—This bread I break—Incarnate devil—
Today, this insect—Out of the sighs—Hold hard, these
ancient minutes—Ears in the turrets hear—And death shall
have no dominion—Altarwise by owl-light—When all my
five and country senses see—After the funeral—The Conversation of Prayer—A Refusal to Mourn—Poem in October—
In My Craft or Sullen Art—Ceremony After a Fire Raid—
Vision and Prayer—Ballad of the Long-Legged Bait—Fern
Hill—Over Sir John's Hill—In the White Giant's Thigh.

The translator is also the author of various translations of
Thomas's work and articles about him that have appeared in
Italian periodicals.

(Portrait of the Artist as a Young Dog)

E. 5 *Ritratto di Giovane Artista*, trans. Lucia Rodocanachi. Torino,
Giulio Einaudi Editore, Apr. 1955, 200 pp., wrappers,
Lire 800.
The edition consisted of 3,600 copies.

SWEDISH

(Portrait of the Artist as a Young Dog)

E. 6 *Porträtt Av Konstnären Som Valp*, trans. Erik Lindegren (the
story 'One Warm Saturday' trans. Thorsten Jonsson).
Stockholm, Albert Bonniers Forläg, 1954, 201 pp., wrappers,
Swedish Crowns 13.50.
The edition consisted of 2,200 copies.

DANISH

(Portrait of the Artist as a Young Dog)

F. 7 *Portraet Af Kunstneren Som Hvalp*, trans. Jørgen Andersen.
København, Gyldendalske Boghandel, Nov. 1955, 184 pp.,
wrappers, D.Kr. 8.75; half-bound, D.Kr. 12.0.

(See plate facing p. 89.)

Gramophone Recordings by, and of Work by, Dylan Thomas

F. 1   *Pleasure Dome*, A Collection of Phonograph Records of Various Poets Reading Their Own Works, ed. Lloyd Frankenberg. Columbia Records Inc., MM–877 (12″, speed 78), 1948.

      Thomas reading 'Poem in October' ('It was my thirtieth year to heaven') and 'In my craft or sullen art.'

F. 2   *Dylan Thomas*. Caedmon Publishers, TC 1002 (12″, L.P.), 1952.

      Thomas reading (side 1) 'Fern Hill' and 'A Child's Christmas in Wales,' and (side 2) 'Do not go gentle into that good night,' 'In the White Giant's Thigh,' 'Ballad of the Long-Legged Bait,' and 'Ceremony after a Fire Raid.' Recorded in New York on 22nd Feb. 1952.

F. 3   *Dylan Thomas*. Caedmon Publishers, TC 1018 (12″, L.P.), 1953.

      Thomas reading (side 1) 'Lament,' 'Poem on His Birthday,' 'Should lanterns shine,' 'There was a saviour,' and 'A Refusal to Mourn . . . ,' and (side 2) 'If I were tickled by the rub of love,' 'And death shall have no dominion,' and 'A Winter's Tale.' Recorded in New York on 2nd June 1953.

F. 4   *Homage to Dylan Thomas*. Argo, R.G.29 (L.P.), 1954. Louis MacNeice—'Requiem Canto,' Hugh Griffith— excerpt from 'Return Journey,' Richard Burton—'Poem in October,' (side 2) Emlyn Williams—'A Visit to Grandpa's,' and Richard Burton—'Fern Hill.' Recorded at the Globe Theatre, London, in collaboration with the Group Theatre.

F. 5   *Under Milk Wood: A Play for Voices by Dylan Thomas*. Argo (two records), R.G.21 and 22 (L.P.), 1954.

      A recording, with the co-operation of the British Broadcasting Corporation, of Douglas Cleverdon's production of the play as broadcast in Jan. 1954.

F. 6   *Dylan Thomas: Fifteen Poems.*   Argo, R.G. 43 (L.P.), 1955.

Richard Burton reading (side 1) 'In My Craft or Sullen Art,' 'The Force That Through the Green Fuse Drives the Flower,' 'A Winter's Tale,' 'The Hand That Signed the Paper,' 'Ballad of the Long-Legged Bait'; (side 2) 'Fern Hill,' 'The Hunchback in the Park,' 'Deaths and Entrances,' 'Before I Knocked,' 'I See the Boys of Summer,' 'Lament,' 'Lie Still, Sleep Becalmed,' 'Do Not Go Gentle into That Good Night,' 'Poem in October,' and 'And Death Shall Have No Dominion.'

Index

NOTE: In this index items printed in roman capitals indicate titles of books by Dylan Thomas, items in italic capitals representing other books. Titles and first lines of individual poems or prose pieces are printed in roman lower case enclosed within quotation marks, whilst periodicals are denoted by italic lower case. Reference numbers in italics denote main entries.

BEST SHORT STORIES OF 1935, THE:
  English and American, D. 2; C. 49
'Birthday Poem,' A. 71; C. 113
Bokanowski, Hélène, A. 3, 8, 44, 64;
  C. 142, 145
Bookman, The, C. 47a
Books (Journal of the National Book
  League), C. 182
Botteghe Oscure, A. 107, 108, 109, 110;
  B. 21; C. 166, 169, 172, 175, 190
Bowen, Elizabeth, D. 3
'Bows glided down, and the coast,
  The,' A. 88; C. 138; D. 11
Boyle, Kay, C. 110
Bozman, E. F., C. 182
Brande, Dorothea, C. 62
'Brember,' C. 14
Bridie, James, B. 19
Brierley, Walter, C. 110
Brinnin, John Malcolm, A. 113;
  C. 185, 196; D. 22
British Broadcasting Corporation,
  B. 23; F. 4
Browne, Douglas G., C. 59
Bullett, Gerald, C. 193
'Burning Baby, The,' B. Intro., 5, 11,
  28; C. 79; D. 7
BURNING BABY, THE, B. *Intro.*
Burton, Miles, C. 59, 70
Burton, Richard, F. 5, 6
Butts, Mary, C. 110

Caetani, Marguerite, C. 190
Caldwell, Erskine, C. 122
'Callous Stars, The,' C. 15
Cambridge Front, A. 83; C. 133
Campbell, Roy, C. 174, 183, 196
'Captain Bigger's Isle,' C. 13
Caravel, A. 42; C. 76
Carr, John Dickson, C. 58
'Cartoon of slashes on the tide-traced
  crater,' A. 36; B. 3; C. 67
Caseg Broadsheet, A. 64; B. 8
'Ceremony After a Fire Raid,' A. 93;
  B. 10, 11; C. 146; D. 12; E. 4;
  F. 2
Chamberlain, Brenda, B. 8

Chance, John Newton, C. 62
'Child's Christmas in Wales, A,'
  B. 24; C. 164; F. 2
'Child's Christmas in Wales, A,' B. 30
'Child's Memories of Christmas in
  Wales, A,' C. 170
'Children's Hour, or Why the B.B.C.
  Broke Down,' C. 13
Christie, Agatha, C. 70
Circus, C. 167, 168
Clare, John, C. 51
Cleverdon, Douglas, F. 4
'A cold, kind man brave in his narrow
  pride,' A. 113; D. 21
COLLECTED POEMS (1st ed., ordinary
  issue), B. 16
—— (1st ed., limited issue), B. 17
—— (American ed.), B. 18
—— (Readers Union ed.), B. 16, 25
Comment, A. 41; C. 69, 73
Connolly, Cyril, C. 158; D. 20
Contemporary Poetry and Prose, A. 16,
  44, 45, 46; C. 79, 82, 85, 92
'Conversation About Christmas,'
  B. 24, 26, 29; C. 164, 170
CONVERSATION ABOUT CHRISTMAS,
  B. 26; C. 164
'Conversation of Prayer(s), The,'
  A. 102; B. 10, 11; C. 152, 154, E. 4
'Cost of Letters, The,' D. 20
'Countryman's Return, The,' A. 83;
  C. 133
Criterion, The, A. 14, 68; C. 41, 49, 81,
  108
Crofts, Freeman Wills, C. 74
'Crumbs of One Man's Year, The,'
  B. 23, 24; C. 162
Curtis, Robert, C. 55

Dalton, Moray, C. 72
Daly, Carroll John, C. 65
Dane, J. Y., C. 58
Davenport, John, C. 183
Davies, Aneirin Talfan, B. 23, 25;
  C. 188
Davy, Colin, C. 71
'De la Mare, Walter,' D. 15

POETRY SINCE 1939, A. 98
POETS AT WORK, A. 88, D. 16a
'Poets of Swansea, The,' C. 16
PORTRAIT OF THE ARTIST AS A YOUNG
   DOG (1st ed.), B. 6; C. 98, 109,
   123, 124, 127, 128, 130
PORTRAIT OF THE ARTIST AS A YOUNG
   DOG (American ed.), B. 7
—— (Guild Books ed.), B. 12
—— (French ed.), E. 1
—— (American cheap ed.), B. 31
—— (Italian ed.), E. 5
—— (Swedish ed.), E. 6
—— (Danish ed.), E. 7
'Process in the weather of the heart,
   A,' A. 6; B. 1, 2, 11, 13; C. 31
Programme, A. 29, 30; C. 60
Prokosch, Frederic, C. 129
'Prologue,' A. 112; B. 16; C. 178
'Prologue to an Adventure,' B. Intro.,
   5, 28; C. 93
'Prospect of the Sea, A,' B. Intro., 5,
   11, 28, 29; C. 91
PROSPECT OF THE SEA, A, B. 4, 26, 28;
   C. 164, 167
'Pub Survey' (review of), C. 107
Purpose, A. 43, 58, 59; C. 77, 88

'Questionnaire: The Cost of Letters,'
   C. 158; D. 20
'Quite Early One Morning,' B. 21, 23,
   24; C. 159
QUITE EARLY ONE MORNING (English ed.), A. 25, 90; B. 23; C. 24,
   143, 157, 159, 160, 161, 162, 165,
   189, 192, 193; D. 15
QUITE EARLY ONE MORNING (American ed.), B. 24, 29; C. 144, 164,
   167, 170, 181; D. 15

Radice, Sheila, C. 100
Readers News, B. 25
Readers Union, B. 25
Reavey, George, B. Intro.
'Refusal to Mourn the Death, by Fire,
   of a Child in London, A,' A. 99;
B. 10, 11, 13; C. 150, 155; D. 13;
E. 4; F. 3
'Reminiscences of Childhood,' A. 25,
   90; B. 23, 24; C. 143, 191
'Replies to an Enquiry,' B. 24; C. 42
'Request to an Obliging Poet,' C. 11
'Request to Leda,' A. 92; B. 9;
   C. 141; D. 17
'Return Journey,' B. 23, 24; C. 192;
   F. 5
Rhode, John, C. 58
Roberts, Denys Kilham, D. 1, 4
Roche, Arthur Somers, C. 61
Rodman, Selden, D. 13
Rodocanachi, Lucia, E. 5
'Roundabouts, The,' B. Intro.
Rudge, William, B. 9

'Saint about to fall, A,' A. 73; B. 4, 11;
   C. 117
Salt, Sydney, C. 40
Sanesi, Roberto, E. 4
Sayers, Dorothy L., C. 65
'School for Witches, The,' B. Intro.,
   5, 28; C. 85; D. 7
'School Memories by a Very Old
   "Boy,"' C. 5
Scott, Sutherland, C. 75
Scottish Bookman, The, A. 28, C. 57
Scurfield, George, C. 133
Searle, Ronald, C. 167, (168)
'See, on gravel paths under the harp-
   strung trees,' A. 25; C. 52
'Seed-at-zero shall not storm, The,'
   A. 51; B. 3
SELECTED WRITINGS, B. 11
Seven, A. 69, 70, 77, 78, 79; C. 112,
   120, 125; 130
'Shall gods be said to thump the
   clouds,' A. 52; B. 3
Shapiro, K., D. 16a
'Should lanterns shine, the holy face,'
   A. 39; B. 3; C. 68; F. 3
'Sidney, Sir Philip,' B. 23, 24
'Sincerest Form of Flattery, The,'
   C. 15
Sitwell, Edith, A. 31; C. 183; D. 17

Valk, Gordon, *C. 71*

Van Dine, S. S., *C. 66*

'Verse of James Chapman Woods,' *C. 20*

'Vest, The,' B. 28; *C. 121*

'Vision and Prayer,' *A. 96*; B. 10, 11; C. 148; E. 4

'Visit to America, A,' B. 23, 24; *C. 189*

'Visit to Grandpa's, A,' B. 6; *C. 98*; F. 5

'Visitor, The,' B. Intro., 4, 5, 28, 29; *C. 49*; D. 2

Vogue, C. 192

Voice of Scotland, The, A. 69; *C. 114*

Von Hutten, Baroness, *C. 72*

Wade, Henry, *C. 65*

Wahl, Jean, A. 54

'Waking alone in a multitude of loves when morning's light,' *A. 91*; C. 140

Wales, A. 62, 63, 74, 75; *C. 93, 94, 97, 102, 118, 127, 144, 159*

'Wales and the Artist,' B. 23, 24

WAR AND THE POET, A. 99; *D. 13*

WAR POETS, THE, A. 93, 97; *D. 12*

'Was there a time when dancers with their fiddles,' *A. 50*; B. 3; *C. 86*

'Watchers, The,' *C. 3*

Watkins, Vernon, *A. 113*; B. 30; C. 195

'We lying by seasand, watching yellow,' *A. 60*; B. 4; C. 89; D. 4

Wells, H. G., *C. 111*

'Welsh Poets,' B. 23, 24

WELSH SHORT STORIES, C. 81; *D. 3*

Western Mail, C. 2a

Whaley, F. J., *C. 75*

'What is the metre of the dictionary?', *A. 34*; B. 3; *C. 67*

Wheatley, Dennis, *C. 63*

'When all my five and country senses

see,' *A. 67*; B. 4, 11, 13; C. 105; E. 4

'When I was a windy boy and a bit,' *A. 110*; C. 172

'When I woke, the town spoke,' *A. 79*; B. 9, 10; *C. 125*

'When, like a running grave, time tracks you down,' *A. 20*; B. 1, 2, 11

'When once the twilight locks no longer,' *A. 11*; B. 1, 2, 11; C. 37

'When the morning was waking over the war,' *A. 89*; C. 139

'Where once the waters of your face,' *A. 9*; B. 1, 2; C. 35; E. 4

'Where Tawe Flows,' *B. 6*

'Who | are you |,' *A. 96*; C. 148

'Who Do You Wish Was With Us?,' *B. 6*

'Why east wind chills and south wind cools,' *A. 47*; B. 3; C. 83

Williams, Emlyn, *F. 5*

Williams, Oscar, C. 194; *D. 8, 11, 12, 19*

Williams, William Carlos, *C. 99*

'Winter's Tale, A,' *A. 103*; B. 10, 11, 13; C. 153; F. 3, 6

'Within his head revolved a little world,' *A. 5*; C. 30

'Woman Speaks, The,' *A. 7*; C. 32

'Woman wails her dead among the trees, A,' *C. 24*

WORLD I BREATHE, THE, *B. 5, 28*; C. 79, 85, 91, 92, 93

World Review, A. 111; *C. 173, 177*

YEAR'S POETRY, THE (1934), A. 8; B. 1; *D. 1*

YEAR'S POETRY, 1937, THE, A. 60, 61; *D. 4*

YEAR'S POETRY, 1938, THE, A. 64

Yellowjacket, C. 38, *121*

'Your breath was shed,' *A. 95*; C. 147, C. 196; D. 16